PANCREATIC CANCER — NEW HOPE
With Orthodox and Alternative Treatment

Preface

This book will prove life saving for the patients suffering from Pancreatic Cancer. He can understand the disease in detail and choose a suitable treatment for them. This book provides simple approach about the clinical symptoms, complications, diagnosis, staging and treatments.

In this book, I have written in detail about Orthodox and Alternative Treatment (Budwig Protocol, which is the best alternative treatment and gives 90% success). Patient can carefully select the right treatment for him. This book has up to date information.

Dr. O.P.Verma

Written by
Dr. O.P.Verma
M.B.B.S., M.R.S.H. (London)
Budwig Wellness
7-B-43, Mahaveer Nagar III, Kota (Raj.)
https://gobudwig.com
+919460816360

Table of Content

Pancreas

The pancreas, named for the Greek words "pan" (all) and "kreas" (flesh), is a 12-15–cm long comma-shaped, soft, lobulated, retroperitoneal organ. It lies transversely, although a bit obliquely, on the posterior abdominal wall behind the stomach, across the lumbar (L1-2) spine.

Gross Anatomy

The pancreas is arbitrarily divided into head, uncinate process, neck, body and tail. The pancreatic head constitutes about 50% and the body and tail the remaining 50% of the pancreatic parenchymal mass. The pancreas weighs about 80gms.

The pancreas is a prismoid in shape and appears triangular in cut section with superior, inferior, and anterior borders as well as anterosuperior, anteroinferior, and posterior surfaces. On the cut surface of the pancreas at its neck, the main pancreatic duct lies closer to the superior border and the posterior surface.

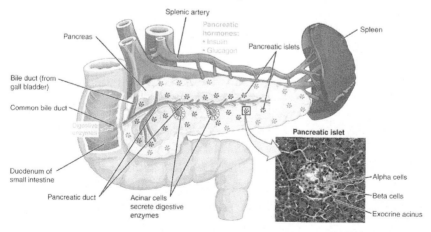

The head of the pancreas lies in the duodenal C loop in front of the inferior vena cava (IVC) and the left renal vein. The uncinate process is an extension of the lower (inferior) half of the head toward the left; it is of varying size and is wedged between the superior mesenteric vessels (vein on right, and artery on left) in front and the aorta behind it.

The lower (terminal) part of the common bile duct runs behind (or sometimes through) the upper half of the head of pancreas before it joins the main pancreatic duct of Wirsung to form a common channel (ampulla), which opens at the papilla on the medial wall of the second part of the duodenum.

The neck of the pancreas lies in front of the superior mesenteric vein, splenic vein and portal vein junction. The body and tail of the pancreas run obliquely upward to the left in front of the aorta and left kidney. The pancreatic neck is the arbitrary junction between the head and body of the pancreas. Portal vein lies behind the neck of the pancreas; no tributaries drain from the posterior surface of the pancreas into the anterior surface of the portal vein; therefore, a tunnel can be easily created behind the neck of the pancreas before its division. The narrow tip of the pancreas tail reaches the splenic hilum in the splenorenal (lienorenal) ligament.

The duodenum (25 cm long) is horseshoe-shaped, with its inferior limb longer than the superior, and has 4 parts: (1) superior (5 cm) at the level of L1; (2) descending, or C loop (7.5 cm), at L1-L3; (3) horizontal, or transverse (10 cm), at L3; and (4) ascending (2.5 cm), leading to the duodenojejunal flexure (junction).

The transverse mesocolon (with the middle colic vessels in it) is attached to the anterior surface of the lower (inferior) part of body and pancreas tail; thus, most of the gland is located in the supracolic compartment. The body and tail of the pancreas lie in the lesser sac (omental bursa) behind the stomach.

Blood supply

Pancreas derives a rich blood supply from both celiac axis and superior mesenteric artery, with collaterals between the two systems; that is why when angiography is done for bleeding as a complication of acute pancreatitis, chronic pancreatitis or pancreatoduodenectomy both celiac axis and superior mesenteric artery should be evaluated.

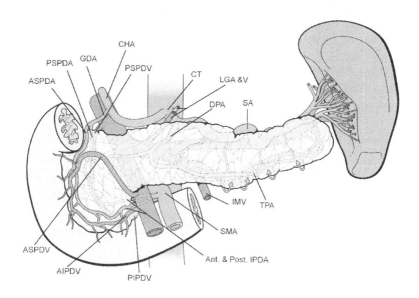

The celiac trunk (axis) comes off from the anterior surface of the aorta at the level of T12–L1. It has a short length of about 1 cm and trifurcates into the common hepatic artery (CHA), splenic artery, and left gastric artery (LGA). The CHA runs toward the right on the superior border of the proximal body of the pancreas, and the splenic artery runs toward the left on the superior border of the distal body and tail of the pancreas.

The superior mesenteric artery (SMA) comes off from the anterior surface of the aorta just below the origin of the celiac trunk at the level of L1 behind the neck of the pancreas. Then, it descends down in front of the uncinate process and the third (horizontal) part of the duodenum to enter the small bowel mesentery.

The gastroduodenal artery (GDA), a branch of the CHA, runs down behind the first part of the duodenum in front of the neck of the pancreas and divides into the right gastro-omental (gastroepiploic) artery (RGEA) and superior pancreaticoduodenal artery (SPDA), which further bifurcates into anterior and posterior branches. The inferior pancreaticoduodenal artery (IPDA) arises from the SMA and also bifurcates into anterior and posterior branches.

The anterior and posterior branches of the SPDA and IPDA join each other and form anterior and posterior pancreaticoduodenal arcades in the anterior and posterior pancreaticoduodenal grooves supplying small branches to the pancreatic head and uncinate process of the pancreas as well as the first, second, and third parts of the duodenum (vasa recta duodeni). Multiple pancreatic branches (including a dorsal pancreatic artery, great pancreatic artery or arteria magna pancreatica) of the splenic artery supply the pancreatic body and tail. Multiple, small pancreatic branches of a dorsal pancreatic artery from the splenic artery and an inferior pancreatic artery from the superior mesenteric artery supply the body and tail of pancreas.

The arterial supply of the pancreas forms an important collateral circulation between the celiac axis and superior mesenteric artery.

Veins accompany the SPDA and IPDA. Superior pancreaticoduodenal veins (SPDVs) drain into the portal vein and inferior pancreaticoduodenal veins (IPDVs) drain into the superior mesenteric vein (SMV). A few small, fragile uncinate veins drain directly into the SMV. Some veins from the head of the pancreas drain into the gastrocolic trunk. Numerous small, fragile veins drain directly from the pancreatic body and tail into the splenic vein.

The SMV lies to the right of the SMA in front of the uncinate process and the third part of the duodenum. The splenic vein arises in the splenic hilum behind the tail of the pancreas and runs from left to right on the posterior surface of the pancreatic body. Union of the horizontal splenic vein and the vertical SMV forms the portal vein behind the neck of the pancreas.

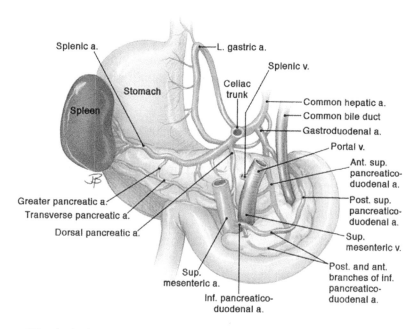

The inferior mesenteric vein (IMV) joins the splenic vein (or the junction of the splenic vein and SMV, or even SMV). The portal vein receives the SPDVs, right gastro-omental (gastroepiploic) vein, left gastric vein (LGV), and right gastric vein (RGV); then, it runs up (superiorly) behind the first part of the duodenum in the hepatoduodenal ligament behind (posterior to) the common bile duct on the right and proper hepatic artery on the left. The portal venous system (splenic vein, SMV, and portal vein) has no valves.

Lymphatic drainage

The head of the pancreas drains into pancreaticoduodenal lymph nodes and lymph nodes in the hepatoduodenal ligament, as well as prepyloric and postpyloric lymph nodes. The pancreatic body and tail drain into mesocolic lymph nodes (around the middle colic artery) and lymph nodes along the hepatic and splenic arteries. Final drainage occurs into celiac, superior mesenteric, and para-aortic and aortocaval lymph nodes.

Nerve supply

The pancreas receives parasympathetic nerve fibres from the posterior vagal trunk via its celiac branch. Sympathetic supply comes from T6-T10 via the thoracic splanchnic nerves and the celiac plexus.

Microscopic Anatomy

Pancreas, compound gland that discharges digestive enzymes into the gut and secretes the hormones insulin and glucagon, vital in carbohydrate (sugar) metabolism, into the bloodstream.

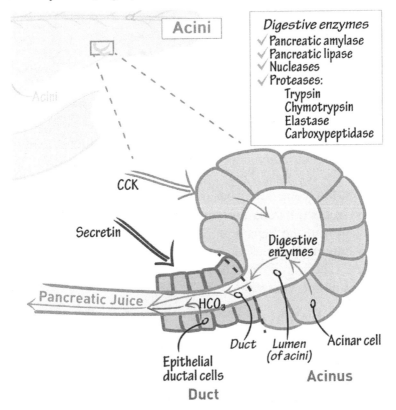

The cells in the pancreas that produce digestive enzymes are called acinar cells (from Latin acinus, meaning "grape"), so named because the cells aggregate to form bundles that resemble a cluster of grapes. Located between the clusters of acinar cells are scattered patches of another type of secretory tissue, collectively known as the islets of Langerhans, named for the 19th-century German pathologist Paul Langerhans. The islets carry out the endocrine functions of the pancreas, though they account for only 1 to 2 percent of pancreatic tissue.

A large main duct, the duct of Wirsung, collects pancreatic juice and empties into the duodenum. In many individuals a smaller duct (the duct of Santorini) also empties into the duodenum. Enzymes active in the digestion of carbohydrates, fat, and protein continuously flow from the pancreas through these ducts. Their flow is controlled by the vagus nerve and by the hormones secretin and cholecystokinin, which are produced in the intestinal mucosa. When food enters the duodenum, secretin and cholecystokinin are released into the bloodstream by secretory cells of the duodenum. When these hormones reach the pancreas, the pancreatic cells are stimulated to produce and release large amounts of water, bicarbonate, and digestive enzymes, which then flow into the intestine.

Secretory function of pancreas:

1- Acinar cells of the exocrine pancreas - secrete the pancreatic digestive enzymes (Inactive enzymes)
2- Duct cells of the exocrine pancreas - secrete large volumes of sodium bicarbonate solution (Alkaline)

Pancreatic juice is composed of two secretory products critical to proper digestion: digestive enzymes and bicarbonate. The enzymes are synthesized and secreted from the exocrine acinar cells, whereas bicarbonate is secreted from the epithelial cells lining small pancreatic ducts. This is a colorless, odourless, and isosmotic alkaline fluid.

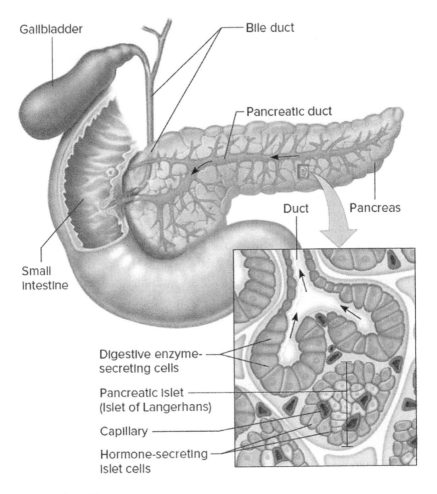

Gallbladder

Bile duct

Pancreatic duct

Duct   Pancreas

Small
Intestine

Digestive enzyme-
secreting cells

Pancreatic Islet
(Islet of Langerhans)

Capillary

Hormone-secreting
Islet cells

Digestive Enzymes

The pancreas secretes a magnificent array of enzymes that collectively have the capacity to reduce virtually all digestible food molecules into forms that are capable of, or nearly capable of being absorbed. Three major groups of enzymes are critical to efficient digestion:

Proteases

Digestion of proteins is initiated by pepsin in the stomach, but the bulk of protein digestion is due to the pancreatic proteases. Several proteases are synthesized in the pancreas and secreted into the lumen of the small intestine. The two major pancreatic proteases are trypsin and chymotrypsin, which are synthesized and packaged into secretory vesicles as the inactive proenzymes trypsinogen and chymotrypsinogen.

Once trypsinogen and chymotrypsinogen are released into the lumen of the small intestine, they must be converted into their active forms in order to digest proteins. Trypsinogen is activated by the enzyme enterokinase, which is embedded in the intestinal mucosa.

Once trypsin is formed it activates chymotrypsinogen, as well as additional molecules of trypsinogen. The net result is a rather explosive appearance of active protease once the pancreatic secretions reach the small intestine.

Trypsin and chymotrypsin digest proteins into peptides and peptides into smaller peptides, but they cannot digest proteins and peptides to single amino acids. Some of the other proteases from the pancreas, for instance carboxypeptidase, have that ability, but the final digestion of peptides into amino acids is largely the effect of peptidases on the surface of small intestinal epithelial cells.

Lipase

A major component of dietary fat is triglyceride, or neutral lipid. A triglyceride molecule cannot be directly absorbed across the intestinal mucosa. Rather, it must first be converted into a monoglyceride and two free fatty acids by the enzyme lipase, is delivered into the lumen of the gut as a constituent of pancreatic juice.

Sufficient quantities of bile salts must also be present in the lumen of the intestine in order for lipase to efficiently digest dietary triglyceride and for the resulting fatty acids and monoglyceride to be absorbed. This means that normal digestion and absorption of dietary fat is critically dependent on secretions from both the pancreas and liver.

Amylase

The major dietary carbohydrate is starch, a storage form of glucose in plants. Amylase is the enzyme that converts starch to maltose (a glucose-glucose disaccharide), as well as the trisaccharide maltotriose. The major source of amylase in all species is pancreatic secretions, although amylase is also present in saliva.

Other Pancreatic Enzymes

In addition to the proteases, lipase and amylase, the pancreas produces a host of other digestive enzymes, including ribonuclease, deoxyribonuclease, phospholipase and cholesterase.

Bicarbonate and Water

Epithelial cells in pancreatic ducts are the source of the bicarbonate and water secreted by the pancreas. Bicarbonate is a base and critical to neutralizing the acid coming into the small intestine from the stomach. The mechanism underlying bicarbonate secretion is essentially the same as for acid secretion by parietal cells in the stomach and is dependent on the enzyme carbonic anhydrase. In pancreatic duct cells, the bicarbonate is secreted into the lumen of the duct and hence into pancreatic juice.

Endocrine Pancreas

The endocrine pancreas consists of the islets of Langerhans. There are approximately one to two million islets that weigh about 1 gram in total and are scattered throughout the pancreas. The pancreatic islets each contain four varieties of cells:

Alpha Cells - The alpha cell, scattered in periphery of the cluster, produces the hormone glucagon and makes up approximately 20 percent of each islet. Glucagon is a 29-amino acid peptide hormone, which plays an important role in blood glucose regulation; low blood glucose levels stimulate its release.

Beta Cells - Approximately 75 percent of the cells in each islet are insulin-producing beta cells, which are clustered centrally in the islet. Elevated blood glucose levels stimulate the release of insulin.

Delta Cells - The delta cell accounts for four percent of the islet cells and secretes the peptide hormone somatostatin. Recall that somatostatin is also released by the hypothalamus (as GHIH), and the stomach and intestines also secrete it. Pancreatic somatostatin, an inhibiting hormone, inhibits the release of both glucagon and insulin.

PP (or F) cells - The PP cell accounts for about one percent of islet cells and secretes the pancreatic polypeptide hormone. It is thought to play a role in appetite, as well as in the regulation of pancreatic exocrine and endocrine secretions. Pancreatic polypeptide is released following a meal may reduce further food consumption; however, it is also released in response to fasting.

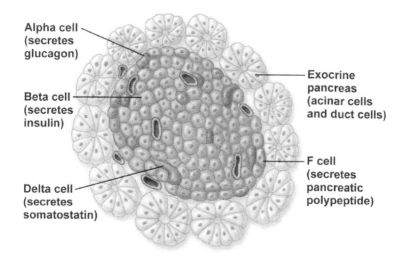

Glucagon

• Glucagon is the principal hyperglycemic hormone, and acts as a counterbalancing hormone to insulin.

• Receptors in the pancreas can sense the decline in blood glucose levels, such as during periods of fasting or during prolonged labour or exercise. In response, the alpha cells of the pancreas secrete the hormone glucagon

- It stimulates the liver to convert its stores of glycogen back into glucose. This response is known as glycogenolysis. The glucose is then released into the circulation for use by body cells.

- It stimulates the liver to take up amino acids from the blood and convert them into glucose. This response is known as gluconeogenesis.

- It stimulates lipolysis, the breakdown of stored triglycerides into free fatty acids and glycerol. Some of the free glycerol released into the bloodstream travels to the liver, which converts it into glucose. This is also a form of gluconeogenesis.

- Taken together, these actions increase blood glucose levels. The activity of glucagon is regulated through a negative feedback mechanism; rising blood glucose levels inhibit further glucagon production and secretion.

Insulin

- Insulin is composed of two peptide chains referred to as the A chain and B chain, with a molecular weight of 6000. A, and B chains are linked together by two disulfide bonds, and an additional disulfide is formed within the A chain. The A chain consists of 21 amino acids and the B chain of 30 amino acids.

- Insulin was the first peptide hormone discovered. Frederick Banting and Charles Herbert Best, working in the laboratory of J. J. R. Macleod at the University of Toronto, were the first to isolate insulin from dog pancreas in 1921

- Frederick Sanger sequenced the amino acid structure in 1951, which made insulin the first protein to be fully sequenced.

- Insulin is also the first protein to be chemically synthesised and produced by DNA recombinant technology.

- Dysfunction of the production of insulin or target cell resistance to the effects of insulin causes diabetes mellitus, a disorder characterized by high blood glucose levels.

Functions of Insulin

- Insulin reduces blood glucose levels by stimulating glycolysis, the breakdown of glucose for generation of energy.

- It takes up amino acids from the blood, and change them into protein in muscle, and liver.

- It acts on fat (adipose) cells to stimulate the uptake of glucose, and the synthesis of fat, lipogenesis.

- It stimulates liver, and skeletal muscle fibres to take up glucose and change it into glycogen, glycogenesis.

- It inhibits enzymes production that is involved in breaking glycogen back down, inhibiting "gluconeogenesis"; that is, the conversion of fats & proteins into glucose.

- Insulin stimulates production of D.N.A. and R.N.A.

Om Verma

Pancreatic Cancer

The pancreas consists of two types of cells that can give rise to pancreatic cancer. Most pancreatic cancers (adenocarcinomas) begin in cells known as exocrine cells that are responsible for producing digestive enzymes that are secreted into the intestine. Much less common are cancers (neuroendocrine tumors) that arise in endocrine cells that produce hormones, including glucagon, insulin, etc. that regulate blood sugar in the body.

Pancreatic cancer is uncommon, but since the majority of these cancers are in the advanced stages at the time of diagnosis, it is the third leading cause of cancer-related deaths in the United States. Treatment options include surgery, chemotherapy, targeted therapies, radiation therapy, and clinical trials.

Causes and Risk Factors of Pancreatic Cancer

The exact causes of pancreatic cancer are not certain, but risk factors may include age, sex, race, genetic factors such as a family history of the disease, and lifestyle issues such as smoking, alcohol use, obesity, and even gum disease.

As symptoms of pancreatic cancer may not arise until it is advanced, it's important to be aware of how these factors may be influencing your own risk so can do what you can to reduce it and have informed conversations with your doctor.

Common Risk Factors

Having a risk factor for pancreatic cancer does not mean that you will develop the disease. These factors do not always "cause" the disease, but rather are more common in people who develop it. Likewise, many people who develop pancreatic cancer do not have any obvious risk factors. Simply understand that, the more risk factors you have, the greater the likelihood you may face pancreatic cancer at some time in your life.

The American Gastroenterological Association recommends that patients who are deemed to be "high risk," including those with a first-degree family history of the disease, and certain genetic diseases, and mutations, be screened for pancreatic cancer. Screening includes genetic testing, counselling and should be conducted in people at least 50 years of age or 10 years younger than the familial onset.

Risk factors may include:

Age

The risk of pancreatic cancer increases with age, though it is possible to be diagnosed at a young age. At the current time, around 90 percent of people are over age 55 at the time of diagnosis, with the average age at diagnosis being 71.

Race

Pancreatic cancer is more common in blacks than in whites, Asians, or Hispanics, but again, may occur in anyone. People of Ashkenazi Jewish heritage have an increased risk, most likely due to a high rate of BRCA2 gene mutations.

Sex

Pancreatic cancer was historically much more common in men than in women, but the gap is closing. The disease is now only slightly more common in men.

Diabetes

Long-term type 2 diabetes is a risk factor for pancreatic cancer. Diabetes may also occur shortly before the diagnosis, often in people who don't have risk factors for diabetes.

The association between the unexpected onset of diabetes in people over the age of 45 and pancreatic cancer was significant enough in a 2018 study that some physicians now recommend screening if it occurs.

Gum Disease and Tooth Loss

Gum disease, referred to as gingivitis in the first stage and periodontitis in the advanced stage, and was first noted to be a risk factor for pancreatic cancer in 2007.

A 2017 review of studies conducted to date found that people were 75 percent more likely to develop pancreatic cancer if they had periodontitis and 54 percent more likely if they had lost all of their teeth (edentulism).

The reason isn't known for sure, but it's thought that certain bacteria that live in the mouth make an enzyme that causes mutations in one type of gene (p53 gene mutations) that can lead to pancreatic cancer.

Chronic Pancreatitis

A history of chronic pancreatitis may increase the risk of pancreatic cancer, especially in people who smoke. Hereditary pancreatitis often begins in childhood and is associated with a much higher risk of the disease.

Other Medical Conditions

The bacterium Helicobacter pylori (H. pylori) is a well-known cause of stomach cancer, as well as peptic ulcer disease. It's thought that it may also increase the risk of pancreatic cancer. There is some evidence that hepatitis C infections, gallstones, gallbladder surgery, and cirrhosis of the liver may be linked with a higher risk of the disease.

Personal History of Cancer

People who have a personal history of several different types of cancer are more likely to develop pancreatic cancer. Researchers aren't certain if this is related to these other cancers in some way, or if the link is due to common risk factors for these cancers (such as smoking).

Blood Type

People with blood types A, B, and AB appear to have a higher risk of pancreatic cancer than those who have type O blood.

Chemical Exposures

Occupational exposures are thought to cause pancreatic cancers, with the chemicals of greatest concern being chlorinated hydrocarbons and polycyclic aromatic hydrocarbons (PAHs). Workers in which an increased risk has been noted include dry cleaning and female laboratory employees.

Genetics

Roughly 10 percent of pancreatic cancers are considered to be hereditary and related to either a family history of the disease or a specific genetic syndrome.

Family History

People who have a family history of pancreatic cancer are more likely to develop the disease. There is also something referred to as familial pancreatic cancer. A person is considered to have this if two or more first-degree relatives (parent, sibling, or child) or three or more extended family members (aunts, uncles, and cousins) have the disease.

Genetic Syndromes

Genetic syndromes linked to pancreatic cancer are often related to specific genetic mutations. Many of these gene mutations, such as BRCA2 gene mutations, are in genes known as tumor suppressor genes. These genes code for proteins that repair damaged DNA and limit the growth of cells. Syndromes associated with a higher risk include:

- Hereditary breast and ovarian cancer syndrome

- Hereditary pancreatitis

- Peutz-Jeghers syndrome

- Lynch syndrome (hereditary nonpolyposis colorectal cancer, HNPCC)

- Li-Fraumeni syndrome

- Von Hippel Lindau syndrome

- Familial adenomatous polyposis

- Familial atypical multiple mole melanoma (FAMMM) syndrome

- Ataxia telangiectasia

- Multiple endocrine neoplasia type 1 (MEN1) syndrome (neuroendocrine tumors)

- Neurofibromatosis type 1 (neuroendocrine tumors)

Lifestyle Risk Factors

Lifestyle factors can play a significant role in the development of pancreatic cancer and include:

Smoking

Smoking increases the risk of pancreatic cancer two- to three-fold and is thought to be responsible for around a third of these cancers.

Unlike lung cancer, in which the risk persists for a long period of time after a person quits smoking (and never returns to normal), the risk of pancreatic cancer returns almost to normal within five to 10 years of quitting.

Alcohol

Long-term, heavy alcohol use (three or more drinks daily) is associated with an increased risk of pancreatic cancer. The risk may be related to an increased risk of pancreatitis in people who drink excessive amounts of alcohol (especially when combined with smoking) rather than the alcohol itself. Moderate alcohol consumption does not appear to increase the risk.

Obesity

Being overweight or obese raises the risk of pancreatic cancer around 20 percent.

Diet

There is some evidence that a high-fat diet, as well as a diet high in red or processed meat, may be associated with an increased risk of pancreatic cancer, especially when foods are cooked at high temperatures. On the other hand, foods high in folic acid, such as green leafy vegetables, may have a protective effect.

A 2017 analysis of studies on diet and pancreatic cancer found that the Western-type diet was associated with a 24 percent greater chance of developing the disease. Coffee may possibly increase the risk as well.

Sedentary lifestyle

A sedentary lifestyle, such as working a desk job, may increase risk, but it's uncertain at this time.

Symptoms of Pancreatic Cancer

The symptoms of pancreatic cancer may include jaundice, pain in the upper abdomen that radiates into the back, the unexpected onset of diabetes, a hard lump in the upper abdomen, as well as non-specific symptoms such as nausea, weight loss, a loss of appetite, and sometimes depression. Unfortunately, the early symptoms are usually vague and nonspecific, with obvious symptoms—ones that may be more likely to prompt someone to seek professional evaluation—often lacking until the disease is in the advanced stages.

Frequent Symptoms

There are a number of symptoms associated with pancreatic cancer, though many of these are more often caused by less serious conditions. These warning signs can vary depending on whether the cancer is located in the head of the pancreas or the organ's body and tail.

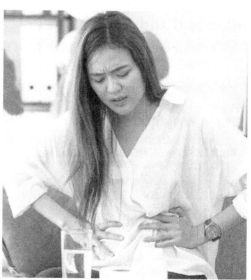

Painless Jaundice

Jaundice, a yellowing discoloration of the skin and the whites of the eyes, is a condition caused by the build-up of bilirubin in the skin and is present in around 30% of people at the time of diagnosis. Bilirubin can accumulate when a pancreatic tumour partially or completely blocks the common bile duct (a duct that carries bile from the liver into the small intestine) and is most common with cancers in the head of the pancreas. With pancreatic cancer, jaundice is usually painless, in contrast to many other causes of jaundice (such as hepatitis or gallstones) that are often associated with pain.

The buildup of bilirubin can also cause stools to become pale and clay-like, as well as a darkening of the urine (cola colored). Stools may also have a strong, odd smell.

Often mistaken for a skin condition, itchy skin (often severe) is also caused by the buildup of bile salts in the skin.

Jaundice can be an early symptom of pancreatic cancers in the head of the pancreas due to obstruction of the bile duct, but may also occur with larger cancers in the tail or body of the pancreas, or if these cancers spread to the liver (liver metastases).

Abdominal and Back Pain

Pain in the mid to upper abdomen that radiates into the back is a common symptom of pancreatic cancer—present in around 70% of people at the time of diagnosis. It is most common with tumors in the tail of the pancreas. This pain often worsens three to four hours after eating or when lying down. In contrast, the pain often lessens when a person sits up and leans forward.

Diarrhea

Diarrhea may occur due to poor absorption in the intestine related to lack of pancreatic enzymes that help digest food. Diarrhea is sometimes an early symptom of pancreatic cancer.

Stools may also have a foul smell, appear frothy or greasy, and float, sometimes making them difficult to flush.

Nausea and Vomiting

Nausea and vomiting are not uncommon in people with pancreatic cancer, although they are frequently misdiagnosed in the early stages of the disease. Severe vomiting may be a sign of an obstruction in the lower part of the stomach (gastric outlet) or upper part of the small intestine (duodenum) caused by pressure from the tumor.

Unintentional Weight Loss

Sudden and unexplained weight loss is very often an indication that something is medically wrong. Explained weight loss, along with a decreased appetite, can be one of the first symptoms of pancreatic cancer. Some people may also notice that they feel full quickly, even when eating a small meal.

Unexpected Diagnosis of Diabetes

The unexpected onset of type 2 diabetes (such as a diagnosis in someone who doesn't have risk factors, such as being overweight) in a person over the age of 45 can be a symptom of pancreatic cancer. It occurs when the pancreas is unable to produce sufficient insulin due to the presence of a tumor.

Blood Clots

Blood clots and cancer can go hand in hand, and sometimes a blood clot is the first sign of the disease. With pancreatic cancer, blood clots may occur in a number of places in the body over time (migratory thrombophlebitis).

Recurrent blood clots without an obvious cause deserve an evaluation.

Abdominal Mass

Some people may notice a hard mass in the upper abdomen—that is actually the gallbladder. The combination of a gallbladder that can be felt and jaundice (if gallstones or a gallbladder infection is not present) is known as Courvoisier's sign. This is a very strong indicator that pancreatic cancer may be present.

Depression

It certainly wouldn't be surprising to become depressed after learning you have pancreatic cancer, but we are learning that depression is sometimes the first symptom of an underlying cancer. Since depression often develops before the diagnosis, it's thought that the biochemical changes associated with the cancer are the primary cause, rather than a reaction to learning about the disease.

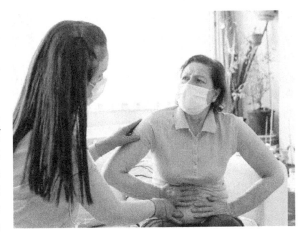

According to a 2017 review of studies, the onset of depression before a diagnosis of pancreatic cancer is much more common than with some other cancers.

Uncommon Symptoms

Symptoms that are uncommon, but sometimes classic for pancreatic cancer, are usually found when the cancer is advanced. These may include:

Enlarged Lymph Node above the Collarbone

An enlarged (swollen) lymph node that can be felt just above the collarbone on the left side (supraclavicular node) may occur. This is referred to medically as Virchow's node.

Mass in the Belly Button

A lump or mass that appears in the belly button (umbilicus) is not uncommon and is referred to as a Sister Mary Joseph nodule.

Paraneoplastic Syndromes

Paraneoplastic syndromes are clusters of symptoms that are related to hormones or other substances that are secreted by cancer cells. One of these syndromes that may be seen with pancreatic cancer includes a combination of tender skin nodules (due to inflammation of the fatty tissue under the skin), inflamed joints (arthritis), and an increased number of a type of white blood cells known as eosinophils.

Rare Pancreatic Tumors

Most pancreatic cancers occur in exocrine cells, which make pancreatic enzymes that aid in digestion. Those that occur in endocrine cells (cells that make hormones) often, but not always, secrete hormones that give rise to the symptoms. Most of these "neuroendocrine" tumors can lead to weight loss. Some of these may include:

Insulinomas

Insulinomas secrete insulin which leads to low blood sugar (hypoglycemia). Symptoms are those of low blood sugar, such as light-headedness, sweating, anxiety, and a rapid heart rate.

Glucagonomas

Glucagonomas secrete glucagon, a hormone that increases blood sugar. This can sometimes cause diabetes, with symptoms of increased thirst, frequent urination, and weight loss being common. They may also cause diarrhea and nutritional deficiencies resulting in mouth and tongue pain.

Gastrinomas

Gastrinomas secrete gastrin, a hormone that can lead to bleeding stomach ulcers (peptic ulcer disease), acid reflux, and abdominal pain.

Somatostatinomas

Somatostatinomas are tumors that secrete somatostatin, a hormone that in turn stimulates the release of other hormones. Symptoms may include diarrhea, abdominal pain, foul-smelling stools, symptoms of diabetes, and jaundice.

VIPomas

VIPomas often secrete vasoactive intestinal peptide (VIP), leading to diarrhea (often very watery and dramatic), nausea, vomiting, abdominal pain and cramping, and flushing of the face and neck.

Om Verma

Complications

Pancreatic cancer can lead to complications for several reasons, including pressure on nearby structures, a lack of substances produced by normal pancreatic cells, the metabolism of cancer itself, or the spread (metastases) from the tumor to other parts of the body.

Specific potential problems may include:

Pancreatic Insufficiency

Pancreatic cancers most often occur in the cells (exocrine cells) that produce pancreatic enzymes. The pancreas ordinarily produces around eight cups of these enzymes daily, which neutralize stomach acid and aid in the breakdown of fats, proteins, and carbohydrates. When a tumor takes over these cells, the lack of enzymes can result in malabsorption, abdominal cramping, and malnutrition, even with a normal diet.

Pancreatic insufficiency occurs in 80% to 90% of people with pancreatic cancer and is treated with pancreatic enzyme replacement.

Bile Duct Obstruction

Obstruction of the common bile duct is a very common complication of pancreatic cancer and may be present at the time of diagnosis. Even when surgery is not possible, a stent can be placed via endoscopy, a procedure that involves inserting a tube into the mouth and threading it down and into the common bile duct.

Stomach or Small Intestine Obstruction

An obstruction caused by the growing tumor may occur either in the area where the contents of the stomach pass into the small intestine (the gastric outlet) or in the first part of the small intestine (the duodenum). If this occurs, a stent can be placed to keep these areas open, or instead, surgery can be done to bypass the obstruction.

Diabetes

As noted above, the sudden and unexpected onset of diabetes may herald the presence of pancreatic cancer.

Even if not present at the time of diagnosis, around 85% of people with the disease will develop insulin resistance or diabetes at some point.

Cachexia

Cancer cachexia, also known as cancer-related anorexia-cachexia syndrome (CACS), is a syndrome that involves weight loss, muscle wasting, and loss of appetite, although it likely begins even before any weight loss occurs. It's thought to be present in up to 80% of people with pancreatic cancer at the time of diagnosis.

Cachexia may be the direct cause of death in 20% of people with cancer. In addition to "normal" cachexia, however, lack of pancreatic enzymes can lead to malnutrition and further weight loss, making this a critical issue to address for anyone diagnosed with pancreatic cancer.

Blood Clots

As noted, blood clots (deep vein thrombosis) that sometimes break off and travel to the lungs (pulmonary emboli) are not just a complication of pancreatic cancer—they can be the first symptom of it. They are also extremely common at any point with the disease. People with pancreatic cancer are also more likely to develop bleeding on blood thinners than people with other types of cancer, so treatment needs to be carefully monitored.

Pain

Pain related to pancreatic cancer can be very severe, but there are a number of different options for controlling cancer pain. Often times, a number of different modalities are combined, such as pain medications, radiation therapy to the abdomen, and a "celiac block," a procedure that blocks the nerves to the abdomen that transmit pain signals to the brain. With the current opioid crisis, it's recommended that people with pancreatic cancer consider a consultation with a pain or palliative care specialist to ensure they receive safe, adequate, and timely pain medication when needed.

When to visit a Doctor

If you notice any of the symptoms above, see your doctor right away. Many of the symptoms of early pancreatic cancer have other possible causes, but several of them are very important to diagnose as well. Symptoms are our body's way of telling us that something isn't right. It's important to have an explanation, and if you don't, ask again. If you aren't getting answers, consider getting a second opinion.

Om Verma

Diagnosis

There are several pieces of information doctors look at in order to diagnose pancreatic cancer. Imaging tests may include a special type of abdominal CT scan, endoscopic ultrasound, MRI, or ERCP. Blood tests can look for causes of jaundice as well as tumor markers, while a medical history focusing on risk factors, along with a physical exam, is also important. A biopsy may or may not be needed, depending on other findings. After diagnosis, staging is done to determine the most appropriate treatments for the disease.

Everyone should be aware of the potential warning signs and symptoms of pancreatic cancer so they can seek a medical evaluation as early as possible. Screening may be recommended based on your risk factors.

Labs and Tests

The evaluation for a possible pancreatic cancer usually begins with a careful history and physical exam. Your doctor will ask you questions about any risk factors you may have, including a family history of the disease, and will inquire about your symptoms. He will then perform a physical examination looking at your skin and eyes for evidence of jaundice; examining your abdomen for a possible mass or enlargement of your liver, or any evidence of ascites (build-up of fluid in the abdomen), and checking your records to see if you have lost weight.

Blood test abnormalities with pancreatic cancer are fairly non-specific but are sometimes helpful in making a diagnosis when combined with imaging tests. Tests may include:

- Liver function tests, which are sometimes increased

- A complete blood count (CBC), looking for an elevated platelet count (thrombocytosis) in particular

- A bilirubin test. There are different types of bilirubin, and based on the specific type tested, physicians may gain clues as to the source of any jaundice you have. With obstructive jaundice (due to a pancreatic tumor pushing on the common bile duct), there are elevations in both conjugated and total bilirubin.

Blood sugar is often elevated, as up to 80% of people with pancreatic cancer will develop insulin resistance or diabetes.

Individuals who suffer from a sudden case of inflamed pancreas, also known as pancreatitis, have a higher risk of developing pancreatic cancer. Individuals with sudden-onset pancreatitis will show elevations in serum amylase and serum lipase in screening tests.

Tumor Markers

Tumor markers are proteins or other factors secreted by cancer cells and can be detected via a blood test, among other tests. According to a study, the tumor marker carcinoembryonic antigen (CEA) is elevated in roughly half of the people diagnosed with the disease. CEA is also elevated in several other types of conditions as well. CA 19-9 levels may be tested, but since they are not always elevated and raised levels can also indicate other medical conditions, this is not particularly helpful in making a diagnosis of pancreatic cancer. This result, however, is helpful in deciding if a pancreatic tumor can be removed surgically, and for following the course of treatment.

Neuroendocrine Tumor Blood Tests

Certain blood tests may also be helpful in diagnosing the rare type of pancreatic cancers referred to as neuroendocrine tumors. Unlike most pancreatic tumors, that are composed of cells that make digestive enzymes, these tumors involve endocrine cells that make hormones such as insulin, glucagon, and somatostatin. Measuring levels of these hormones, as well as conducting a few other blood tests, can be helpful in diagnosing these tumors.

Imaging

Imaging tests are usually the primary method of confirming or refuting the presence of a mass in the pancreas. Options may include:

CT Scan

Computerized tomography (CT) uses X-rays to create a cross-section of a region of the body at different levels, and is often the mainstay of diagnosis. If a physician suspects pancreatic cancer specifically, a special type of CT scan called a multiphase helical CT scan or pancreatic protocol CT scan is often recommended.

A CT scan can be helpful both for characterizing the tumor (determining its size and location in the pancreas) and looking for any evidence of spread to lymph nodes or other regions. CT may be more effective than endoscopic ultrasound in determining whether cancer has spread to the superior mesenteric artery (important in choosing treatment).

Endoscopic Ultrasound (EUS)

Ultrasound uses sound waves to create an image of the inside of the body. A conventional (transcutaneous) ultrasound is not usually done if a doctor suspects pancreatic cancer, as intestinal gas can make visualization of the pancreas difficult. But it may be helpful when looking for other abdominal problems.

An endoscopic ultrasound can be a valuable procedure in making the diagnosis. Done via endoscopy, a flexible tube with an ultrasound probe at its end is inserted through the mouth and threaded down into the stomach or small intestine, so that the scan can be done from inside.

Because these areas are very near to the pancreas, the test allows doctors to get a very good look at the organ.

With the use of medications (conscious sedation), people usually tolerate the procedure well. The test may be more accurate than CT for assessing the size and extent of a tumor but isn't as good at finding any distant spread of the tumor (metastases) or determining if the tumor involves blood vessels.

Endoscopic Retrograde Cholangiopancreatography (ERCP)

Retrograde cholangio-pancreatography (ERCP) is a test that involves endoscopy plus X-rays in order to visualize the bile ducts. ERCP can be a sensitive test for finding pancreatic cancer but is not as accurate in differentiating the disease from other problems, such as pancreatitis. It's also an invasive procedure, similar to some of the tests described above.

MRI

Magnetic resonance imaging (MRI) uses magnets rather than X-rays to create an image of internal structures. MRI is used less often than CT with pancreatic cancer but may be used in certain circumstances. As with CT, there are special types of MRI, including MR cholangio-pancreatography (MRCP). Since it hasn't been studied as much as the tests above, it's used primarily for people for whose diagnosis is unclear based on other studies, or if a person has an allergy to the contrast dye used for CT.

Octreoscan

A test called an octreoscan or somatostatin receptor scintigraphy (SRC) may be done if a neuroendocrine tumor of the pancreas is suspected. In an octreoscan, a radioactive protein (called a tracer) is injected into a vein. If a neuroendocrine tumor is present, the tracer will bind to cells in the tumor. Several hours later, a scan (scintigraphy) is done that picks up any radiation that is being emitted (neuroendocrine tumors will light up, if present).

PET-CT Scan

PET scans, often combined with CT (PET/CT), may occasionally be done, but are used much less often with pancreatic cancer than with some other cancers. In this test, a small amount of radioactive sugar is injected into a vein and a scan is done after the sugar has had time to be absorbed by cells.

Actively growing cells, such as cancer cells, will "light up," in contrast to areas of normal cells or scar tissue.

Biopsy

Microscopic examination of tissue (a biopsy) is needed to confirm the diagnosis most of the time, as well as look at the molecular characteristics of the tumor. In selected cases, surgery can be done without a biopsy.

A fine needle biopsy (a procedure in which a thin needle is directed through the skin in the abdomen, and into the pancreas to extract a sample of tissue) is most often done using guidance with either ultrasound or CT.

There is some concern that this type of biopsy could "seed" the tumor, or result in the spread of the cancer along the line where the needle is introduced.

It's not known how often seeding occurs, but according to a 2017 study, the number of case reports of seeding due to endoscopic ultrasound-guided fine needle aspiration has been rapidly increasing.

Since biopsies are done primarily to see if surgery may be done, this is a concern worth talking about with your doctor.

As an alternative approach, laparoscopy may be used, especially if a tumor may be able to be removed (resectable). In a laparoscopy, several small incisions are made in the abdomen and a narrow instrument is inserted to perform the biopsy. This procedure can identify up to 20% of surgery candidates whose tumors are actually inoperable. Some physicians recommend utilizing this type of laparoscopy for anyone who will be having surgery (to avoid unnecessary extensive surgery).

Om Verma

Differential Diagnoses

There are a number of conditions that may mimic the symptoms of pancreatic cancer or result in similar findings on blood tests and imaging. Doctors will work to rule out the following before making a diagnosis:

- **Bile duct stricture**, an abnormal narrowing of the bile duct. It may be caused by gallstones or surgery to remove them, but may also be caused by pancreatic cancer.

- **Acute or chronic pancreatitis**, an inflammation of the pancreas, can cause similar symptoms, but does not result in a mass. Between 7% and 14% of those diagnosed with pancreatic cancer also present with acute pancreatitis.

- **Bile duct stones** in the bile duct can cause symptoms of obstructive jaundice and can often be seen on ultrasound. Like bile duct strictures, however, they may be present along with pancreatic cancer.

- **Ampullary carcinoma**

- **Gallbladder cancers** can appear very similar to pancreatic cancers but may be differentiated with CT or MRI.

- **Gallstones (cholelithiasis)**

- **Gastric or duodenal ulcers**

- **Abdominal aortic aneurysm**

- **Pancreatic lymphoma**

- **Gastric lymphoma**

- **Liver cancer**

- **Bile duct cancer**

Om Verma

Staging

Determining the stage of a pancreatic cancer is extremely important when it comes to deciding whether a cancer can be surgically removed or not. If staging is inaccurate, it may lead to unnecessary surgery. Staging can also assist in estimating the prognosis of the disease.

TNM Staging

Doctors often use a system called TNM staging to determine the stage of a tumor. This can be terribly confusing at first but is much easier to understand if you know what these letters mean.

T stands for tumor. A tumor is given a number from T1 to T4 based on the size of the tumor, as well as other structures the tumor may have invaded. For a primary tumor:

- T1: Tumor confined to the pancreas and less than 2 cm.

- T2: Tumor confined to the pancreas and more than 2 cm.

- T3: Tumor extends beyond the pancreas (to the duodenum, bile duct, or mesenteric vein), but does not involve the celiac axis or superior mesenteric artery.

- T4: Tumor involves the celiac artery or the superior mesenteric artery.

N stands for lymph nodes. N0 would mean that a tumor has not spread to any lymph nodes, meaning there is no involvement of regional lymph nodes. N1 means that the tumor has spread to nearby lymph nodes, meaning regional lymph nodes are positive for cancer.

M stands for metastases. If a tumor has not spread, it would be described as M0, meaning no distant metastasis. If it has spread to distant regions (beyond the pancreas) it would be referred to as M1.

Based on TNM, tumors are then given a stage between 0 and 4. There are also substages:

- Stage 0: Stage 0 is also referred to as carcinoma-in-situ and refers to cancer that has not yet spread past something called the basement membrane. These tumors are not invasive (though subsequent stages are) and should theoretically be completely curable.

- **Stage 1:** Stage 1 (T1 or T2, N0, M0) pancreatic cancers are confined to the pancreas and are less than 4 cm (about 2 inches) in diameter.

- **Stage 2:** Stage 2 tumors (either T3, N0, M0 or T1-3, N1, M0) either extend beyond the pancreas (without involving the celiac axis or superior mesenteric artery) and have not spread to lymph nodes, or are confined to the pancreas but have spread to lymph nodes.

- **Stage 3:** Stage 3 tumors (T4, any N, M0) extend beyond the pancreas and involve either the celiac artery or superior mesenteric artery. They may or may not have spread to lymph nodes, but have not spread to distant regions of the body.

- **Stage 4:** Stage 4 tumors (Any T, any N, M1) can be any size. While they may or may not have spread to lymph nodes, they have spread to distant sites such as the liver, the peritoneum (the membranes that line the abdominal cavity), the bones, or the lungs.

Treatment

Surgery

Pancreatic cancer surgery is a major procedure that can alleviate the effects of pancreatic cancer to improve survival. Sometimes pancreatic cancer can be cured, but often the treatment relieves some aspects of the disease even if a complete cure isn't possible. Management of pancreatic cancer includes surgery, radiation, chemotherapy, and immunotherapy.

Pancreatic cancer surgery includes surgical operations that remove the tumor from the pancreas and surrounding areas. Your procedure can also include clearing blockages in the ducts or other structures around the pancreas.

The pancreas lies just behind the stomach and the duodenum (the entrance of the small intestine). It produces digestive enzymes, so removing it can have a substantial effect on your nutrition. Pancreatic cancer surgery usually involves the removal of some, but not all, of the pancreas whenever possible.

You would have your procedure under general anesthesia. You might have an open procedure or a minimally invasive laparoscopic surgery, depending on the size of the tumor and how widespread your cancer is.

Often, complicated surgeries with multiple areas of cancer or a high risk of bleeding are done with an open procedure. When surgery is done for removal of a small cancer growth without duct blockage or involvement of blood vessels, a laparoscopic operation might be done.

Types of pancreatic cancer surgery include:

- **Whipple procedure:** Also described as pancreatico-duodenectomy, this is the surgical removal of the gallbladder, common bile duct, the head of the pancreas, part of the

41

duodenum, part of the stomach, the spleen, and nearby lymph nodes. The pancreas tail and part of the pancreas body are left to preserve the production of digestive enzymes and hormones.

- **Whipple procedure variations:** There are several modifications to the classic Whipple procedure. These surgeries may preserve more digestive function and help minimize postoperative complications. Variations such as pylorus preserving pancreatico-duodenectomy involve the removal of less of the stomach and/or duodenum.

- **Distal pancreatectomy:** Cancers in the body or tail of the pancreas are seldom operable, but when they are, the tail of the pancreas may be removed with or without the spleen.

- **Total Pancreatectomy:** Total pancreatectomy is essentially the same as a Whipple procedure, but differs in that the entire pancreas is removed.

Whipple procedure

Generally, your surgeon would plan the type of procedure that you are having in advance. But sometimes pancreatic surgery is more widespread than anticipated, and the procedure may change from laparoscopic surgery to an open procedure, or your surgeon might remove more of the pancreas or the intestine than initially planned.

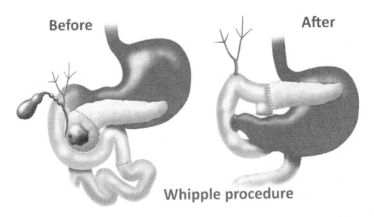

Whipple procedure

Contraindications

Surgery is not always an option if you have pancreatic cancer. Sometimes the cancer is so far advanced that surgery would be expected to reduce life expectancy and diminish quality of life.

And the tumor location can make it inoperable. For example, if your pancreatic cancer has enveloped major blood vessels, the risk of life-threatening bleeding during surgery could mean that you are not a candidate for surgery.

Additionally, very serious health problems, like end-stage liver or heart failure, can make you unlikely to recover after pancreatic cancer surgery and might make an operation too risky for you.

Potential Risks

If you have pancreatic cancer surgery, you will be exposed to the risks of general anesthesia and surgery.

Additional complications that can occur with pancreatic cancer surgery include:

- Life-threatening bleeding
- Infection
- Blood clots
- Gastrointestinal inflammation
- Gastrointestinal blockage
- Digestive problems leading to malnutrition
- Dumping syndrome, with severe weight loss due to diarrhea shortly after eating
- A severe decline in overall health with a reduced quality of life

After a total pancreatectomy, the body doesn't produce insulin, glucagon, or digestive enzymes. Diabetes develops and insulin therapy and enzyme replacement are necessary.

Although it isn't a result of surgery, cancer recurrence is highly likely after pancreatic cancer surgery. The chance that pancreatic cancer will recur after surgery depends on many factors, and your oncologist (cancer doctor) and surgeon will discuss your likelihood of cancer recurrence with you.

Purpose of Pancreatic Cancer Surgery

Pancreatic cancer is fatal if it is untreated. The condition doesn't resolve or improve on its own, and it worsens rapidly. So a treatment plan needs to be considered immediately after diagnosis, or even sooner, such as during the diagnostic process.

Pancreatic cancer can spread locally, obstructing the small intestine, pancreatic and bile ducts, or interfering with blood flow. These issues may cause symptoms and can lead to death.

Treatment is rarely curative, although it can help slow the growth of the tumor, reduce the symptoms, and improve your quality of life. Relieving obstruction due to pancreatic cancer can be highly beneficial even if the cancer isn't cured.

Pancreatic cancer surgery is the better treatment option that can potentially cure the disease. Surgery can also be considered as an option for palliative care to reduce the symptoms of the condition.

In the early stages, pancreatic cancer doesn't typically cause noticeable signs or symptoms. It is usually diagnosed at a late stage when it has already spread within the abdomen or after it has metastasized to distant areas of the body.

Sometimes blood tests may identify high blood sugar or elevated bilirubin, but the condition is generally diagnosed with abdominal imaging tests. If pancreatic cancer is detected incidentally, such as when you have an imaging test for another reason, it is important that you discuss a treatment plan with your doctor promptly.

Pre-Op Lifestyle Changes

You might need to make some dietary adjustments due to your pancreatic cancer. This can include reducing fat intake or managing and timing your carbohydrate intake with insulin doses.

Smoking can interfere with your recovery, and your doctor may suggest that you quit smoking. Keep in mind that you might not have a long wait between your pancreatic cancer diagnosis and your pancreatic cancer surgery, so you might begin smoking cessation before surgery, and you would have to maintain that after your surgery.

How to Prepare

You will need to have an oncologist and a surgeon involved in your pancreatic cancer surgery preparation.

You might have a laparoscopic biopsy before surgery so your tumor can be examined under a microscope for grading and staging. You are likely to have abdominal and chest imaging tests to identify metastatic lesions.

Chemotherapy and radiation therapy are usually part of the treatment for pancreatic cancer.

You might have neoadjuvant chemotherapy, which is a chemotherapy regimen that is given to shrink the tumor before surgery. Similarly, you might have radiation to shrink your tumor before your operation.

Pre-operative testing includes a chest X-ray and electrocardiogram (EKG) and blood tests, such as a complete blood count (CBC), blood chemistry tests, and liver function tests. If your pre-operative diagnostic testing reveals surgical contraindications, your surgery would have to be cancelled.

Your operation will be done in a hospital operating room. Often, pancreatic cancer surgery is done while you are already in the hospital, but you might come in from home for your surgery appointment.

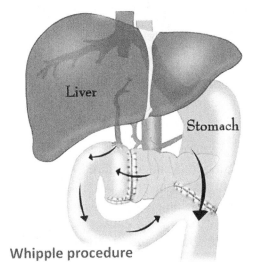

Whipple procedure

You will need to stay in the hospital for at least a few days after your surgery, and possibly for several weeks after your operation.

You can wear anything comfortable when you go to your surgery appointment. You will change into a hospital gown for your surgery and you will also wear a hospital gown while you are staying overnight as an inpatient.

You will have to fast from food and drink after midnight the night before your surgery.

Medications

You will have very specific instructions regarding medication use prior to your surgery. If you have been taking medications such as blood thinners or treatment for diabetes or hypertension prior to your pancreatic cancer diagnosis, the doses may be adjusted for a few days before your surgery.

You might have a few new medications started before your surgery. Chemotherapy could be part of your pre-surgical treatment. And other medications to help manage the symptoms of your pancreatic cancer may include pain medication or insulin. You could still be adjusting to these treatments at the time of your surgery.

What to Expect on the Day of Surgery

If you are coming in from home for your pancreatic cancer surgery, you will have to register and sign a consent form. If you are already an inpatient in the hospital, you will also have to sign a consent form shortly before your operation.

You will have your temperature, blood pressure, pulse, and breathing rate monitored. You will also have your oxygen saturation monitored with a non-invasive pulse oximeter.

You will have blood tests, including CBC, chemistry panel, and liver function tests. You will also have a urinalysis. And you might have same-day imaging tests to identify any changes in your pancreatic cancer, such as a more extensive spread.

If you have not already had an intravenous (IV, in a vein) line in your arm or hand, it will be placed. You may have a urinary catheter placed before you go to the operating room or after you get there.

Your surgeon and anaesthesiologist will likely check on you before you go to the operating room.

In the operation theatre

You will have your anaesthesia started, and your skin cleansed in preparation for surgery. If you have not had a urinary catheter placed, it will be placed when your surgical preparation is in progress.

Your body will be covered with a surgical drape. The area where the incision will be placed will be exposed and cleaned with a surgical cleaning solution.

Your blood pressure, pulse, oxygen saturation, and breathing rate will be continuously monitored. Your anaesthesia will be started as medication is injected in your IV to make you sleep. The medication will also prevent you from feeling pain and will paralyze your muscles.

You will have a breathing tube inserted in your throat so that you will have mechanical assistance for breathing throughout your surgery.

During the Surgery

Your surgeon will begin your surgery by making an incision in your skin. You may have a small incision less than an inch in length for a laparoscopic procedure, or a larger incision if you are having an open laparotomy. Your incision for an open laparotomy will be several inches long, and may vary in size. It could be longer if your surgery will involve your stomach and small intestine.

Your surgeon will then make a deeper incision into your peritoneum, which is the connective tissue that supports and encloses your abdominal organs.

If you are having laparoscopic surgery, the thin laparoscope fitted with light source and camera will be inserted into your abdomen and your surgeon will view the internal structures of your abdominal cavity on a monitor.

Even with the imaging tests we have available, it is not possible to know whether cancer has spread to the point where surgery is inadvisable before the surgery itself is done. During surgery, if your surgeon may discover that your cancer has spread too far for the procedure to be considered a good option, then he may close your incision without removing your pancreas or other structures as previously planned.

Now your surgeon will carefully cut out areas of cancer that can be safely removed. This can mean cutting away a portion of the pancreas, gallbladder, spleen, lymph nodes, and/or small intestine and stomach.

- Often, the blood vessels that had been supplying blood to the resected structures need to be closed off with sutures to prevent bleeding.

- Extensive restructuring can be a major part of this surgery. You may need to have your stomach and small intestine reattached after portions are removed from one or both.

- The ducts that connect the pancreas to the stomach and small intestine may need to be reattached after the organs are cut and restructured.

- If it is not possible for your stomach and small intestine to be immediately reattached due to severe inflammation, you may have an ostomy, which is a pouch that collects fluid. A portion of your intestine would be attached to a bag that extends outside of your skin. Your digestive structures may be reattached at a later date, possibly months after your surgery.

- If substantial post-operative swelling and inflammation are anticipated, you may have a surgical drain placed in your abdomen. This drain would extend outside your skin, and it would be removed several weeks after your surgery.

Your surgeon may also cut away portions of blood vessels or ducts that are invaded by cancer or obstructed by cancer, inflammation, or blood clots. Sometimes a stent (a small artificial tube-shaped metallic or plastic structure) is placed permanently inside the ends of a duct as a bypass keep it open after a section has been cut away.

You may have imaging tests to examine the flow through blood vessels and ducts from which obstruction has been removed. Imaging tests might be done during your surgery to see if there are any leaks that need to be repaired in areas that have been reattached during surgery, like the intestine.

When the cancer is removed, the structures repaired, and the imaging tests have shown that no further repair is necessary, the surgical instruments will be removed. Your peritoneal cavity will be closed, your skin closed, and your wound covered with surgical dressing.

Your anaesthesia will be reversed and the breathing tube will be removed. Your anaesthesia team will ensure that you are breathing comfortably before you go to the recovery area.

After the Surgery

You will be monitored in the recovery area before you will go to the intensive care unit (ICU). You might spend a few days in ICU, before you go to a regular hospital room.

You will get pain medications as needed and your medical team will check on your surgical drain. If you aren't having any major complications (like extensive bleeding), you will go to your hospital room.

Over the next few days, you should be able to start drinking clear fluids and to advance your diet slowly. You will have your urinary catheter removed and you should be able to use the toilet.

Your medical care team will check on your surgical wound, as well as your ostomy and drain. And you continue to receive pain medication as needed.

You may have imaging tests to evaluate the repair. And you might have radiation and or/chemotherapy for treatment of your pancreatic cancer.

If complications, like severe bleeding, a blood clot, an infection, or a bowel obstruction arise, you would need urgent medical and/or surgical intervention. This can prolong your hospital stay.

Before you go home, you will have instructions about how to take care of your wound, drain, and ostomy. You will receive prescriptions for pain medication and any other medications that you need. And you will receive instructions about advancing your diet, complications to look out for, and follow up appointments.

Recovery

As you are recovering from your pancreatic cancer surgery, your cancer care will also be a major aspect of your overall care.

You need to heal from surgery and adapt to any gastrointestinal changes resulting from the surgery.

When you go to see your doctor, you will have your external sutures removed. You may have your drain removed at another visit. And you will continue to have periodic imaging tests to assess your pancreatic cancer as you are undergoing radiation therapy and chemotherapy.

Chemotherapy

Chemotherapy (chemo) is an anti-cancer drug injected into a vein or taken by mouth. These drugs enter the bloodstream and reach almost all areas of the body, making this treatment potentially useful for cancers whether or not they have spread.

When might chemotherapy be used?

Chemo is often part of the treatment for pancreatic cancer and may be used at any stage:

- **Before surgery (neoadjuvant chemotherapy):** Chemotherapy can be given before surgery (sometimes along with radiation) to try to shrink the tumor so it can be removed with less extensive surgery. Neoadjuvant chemotherapy is often used to treat cancers that are too big to be removed by surgery at the time of diagnosis (called locally advanced cancers).

- **After surgery (adjuvant chemotherapy):** Chemotherapy can be used after surgery (sometimes along with radiation) to try to kill any cancer cells that have been left behind or have spread but can't be seen, even on imaging tests. If these cells were allowed to grow, they could form new tumors in other places in the body. This type of treatment might lower the chance that the cancer will come back later.

- **For advanced pancreatic cancer:** Chemotherapy can be used when the cancer is advanced and can't be removed completely with surgery, or if surgery isn't an option, or if the cancer has spread to other organs.

When chemo is given along with radiation, it is known as chemoradiation. It helps the radiation work better, but can also have more side effects.

Which chemo drugs are used for pancreatic cancer?

In most cases (especially as adjuvant or neoadjuvant treatment), chemotherapy is most effective when combinations of drugs are used. For people who are healthy enough, 2 or more drugs are usually given together. For people who are not healthy enough for combined treatments, a single drug (usually gemcitabine, 5-FU, or capecitabine) can be used.

The most common drugs used for both adjuvant and neoadjuvant chemo include:

- Gemcitabine (Gemzar)

- 5-fluorouracil (5-FU)

- Oxaliplatin (Eloxatin)

- Albumin-bound paclitaxel (Abraxane)

- Capecitabine (Xeloda)

- Cisplatin

- Irinotecan (Camptosar)

Chemotherapy for advanced pancreatic cancer

- Gemcitabine (Gemzar)

- 5-fluorouracil (5-FU) or Capecitabine (Xeloda) (an oral 5FU drug)

- Irinotecan (Camptosar) or Liposomal Irinotecan (Onivyde)

- Platinum agents : Cisplatin and Oxaliplatin (Eloxatin)

- Taxanes: Paclitaxel (Taxol), Docetaxel (Taxotere), and Albumin-bound paclitaxel (Abraxane)

How is chemotherapy given?

Chemotherapy drugs for pancreatic cancer can be given into a vein (IV) or by mouth as a pill. The infusion can be done in a doctor's office, chemotherapy clinic, or in a hospital setting.

Often, a slightly larger and sturdier IV is required in the vein system to give chemo. They are known as central venous catheters (CVCs), central venous access devices (CVADs), or central lines. They are used to put medicines, blood products, nutrients, or fluids right into your blood. They can also be used to take out blood for testing.

Doctors give chemo in cycles, with each period of treatment followed by a rest period to give you time to recover from the effects of the drugs. Cycles are most often 2 or 3 weeks long. The schedule varies depending on the drugs used. For example, with some drugs, the chemo is given only on the first day of the cycle. With others, it is given for a few days in a row, or once a week. Then, at the end of the cycle, the chemo schedule repeats to start the next cycle.

Adjuvant and neoadjuvant chemotherapy is often given for a total of 3 to 6 months, depending on the drugs used. The length of treatment for advanced pancreatic cancer is based on how well it is working and what side effects you may have.

Possible side effects

Chemo drugs can cause side effects. These depend on the type and dose of drugs given and how long treatment lasts. Common possible side effects include:

- Nausea and vomiting
- Loss of appetite
- Hair loss

- Mouth sores

- Diarrhea or constipation

Chemo can also affect the blood-forming cells of the bone marrow, which can lead to:

- Increased chance of infection (from low white blood cells)

- Bleeding or bruising (from low platelet counts)

- Fatigue or shortness of breath (from low red blood cells)

These side effects usually go away after treatment is finished. There are often ways to lessen these side effects. For example, drugs can be given to help prevent or reduce nausea and vomiting.

Some chemo drugs can cause other side effects. For example:

- Drugs such as cisplatin, oxaliplatin, and paclitaxel can damage nerves, which can lead to symptoms of numbness, tingling, or even pain in the hands and feet (called peripheral neuropathy). For a day or so after treatment, oxaliplatin can cause nerve pain that gets worse with exposure to cold, including when swallowing cold foods or liquids.

- Cisplatin can damage the kidneys. Doctors try to prevent this by giving the patient lots of intravenous (IV) fluid before and after the drug is given.

- Cisplatin can affect hearing. Your doctor may ask if you have any ringing in the ears or hearing loss during treatment.

Radiation therapy

Radiation therapy is the use of high-energy x-rays or other particles to destroy cancer cells. A doctor who specializes in giving radiation therapy to treat cancer is called a radiation oncologist. The most common type of radiation treatment is called external-beam radiation therapy, which is radiation given from a machine outside the body. Learn more about the basics of radiation therapy.

External-beam radiation therapy is the type of radiation therapy used most often for pancreatic cancer. A radiation therapy regimen, or schedule, usually consists of a specific number of treatments given over a set period of time. There are different ways that radiation therapy can be given:

- **Traditional radiation therapy.** This is also called conventional or standard fraction radiation therapy. It is made up of daily treatments of lower doses of radiation per fraction or day. It is given over 5 to 6 weeks in total.

- **Stereotactic body radiation (SBRT) or cyberknife.** These are shorter treatments of higher doses of radiation therapy given over as few as 5 days. This is a newer type of radiation therapy that can provide more localized treatment in fewer treatment sessions. Whether this approach works as well as traditional radiation therapy is not yet known, and it may not be appropriate for every person. It should only be given in specialized centers with experience and expertise in using this technology for pancreatic cancer and identifying who it will work best for.

- **Proton beam therapy.** This is a type of external-beam radiation therapy that uses protons rather than x-rays. At high energy, protons can destroy cancer cells. It also lessens the amount of healthy tissue that receives radiation. Proton beam therapy may be given for a standard amount of time or for a shorter time like SBRT. It is not yet known whether it works better than standard radiation therapy, and it may not be an option for every person. It should be given in treatment centers that have the experience and skills needed to use this treatment for pancreatic cancer, which may only be available through a clinical trial.

Other types of radiation therapy may also be offered. There are many different ways radiation therapy is given, so it's important to talk with your doctor about their planned approach.

Often, chemotherapy will be given at the same time as radiation therapy because it can enhance the effects of the radiation therapy, which is called radiosensitization. Combining chemotherapy and radiation therapy may occasionally help shrink the tumor enough so it can be removed by surgery. However, chemotherapy given at the same time as radiation therapy often has to be given at lower doses than when given alone.

Radiation therapy may be helpful for reducing the risk of the pancreatic cancer returning or re-growing in the original location. But there remains much uncertainty as to how much, if at all, it lengthens a person's life.

Side effects from radiation therapy may include fatigue, mild skin reactions, nausea, upset stomach, and loose bowel movements. Most side effects go away soon after treatment is finished. Talk with your health care team about what you can expect and how side effects will be managed.

Targeted therapy

Targeted therapy is a treatment that targets the cancer's specific genes, proteins, or the tissue environment that contributes to cancer growth and survival. This type of treatment blocks the growth and spread of cancer cells and limits damage to healthy cells.

Not all tumors have the same targets. To find the most effective treatment, your doctor may run tests to identify the genes, proteins, and other factors in your tumor. This helps doctors better match each patient with the most effective treatment whenever possible. In addition, research studies continue to find out more about specific molecular targets and new treatments directed at them.

- **Erlotinib (Tarceva)** is approved for people with advanced pancreatic cancer in combination with the chemotherapy drug gemcitabine. Erlotinib blocks the effect of the epidermal growth factor receptor (EGFR), a protein that can become abnormal and help cancer grow and spread. The side effects include a skin rash similar to acne, diarrhea, and fatigue.

- **Olaparib (Lynparza)** is approved for people with metastatic pancreatic cancer associated with a germline (hereditary) BRCA mutation. It is intended for use as maintenance therapy after a patient has been on platinum-based chemotherapy, such as oxaliplatin or cisplatin, for at least 16 weeks with no evidence of disease progression.

- **Larotrectinib (Vitrakvi)** is a tumor-agnostic treatment that can be used for any type of cancer that harbours a specific genetic change called an NTRK fusion. This type of genetic change is found in a range of cancers, including pancreatic cancer, though it is rare. It is approved as a treatment for pancreatic cancer that is metastatic or locally advanced and has not responded to chemotherapy.

Talk with your doctor about possible side effects for a specific medication and how they can be managed.

Immunotherapy

Immunotherapy, also called biologic therapy, is designed to boost the body's natural defences to fight the cancer. It uses materials made either by the body or in a laboratory to improve, target, or restore immune system function.

Immune checkpoint inhibitors, which include anti-PD-1 antibodies such as pembrolizumab (Keytruda), are an option for treating pancreatic cancers that have high microsatellite instability (MSI-H). Approximately 1% to 1.5% of pancreatic cancers are associated with high MSI-H.

Different types of immunotherapy can cause different side effects. Common side effects include skin reactions, flu-like symptoms, diarrhea, and weight changes. Talk with your doctor about possible side effects of the immunotherapy recommended for you.

Palliative or supportive care

Cancer and its treatment cause physical symptoms and side effects, as well as emotional, social, and financial effects. Managing all of these effects is called palliative care or supportive care. It is an important part of your care that is included along with treatments intended to slow, stop, or eliminate the cancer.

Palliative care focuses on improving how you feel during treatment by managing symptoms and supporting patients and their families with other, non-medical needs. Any person, regardless of age or type and stage of cancer, may receive this type of care. And it often works best when it is started right after a cancer diagnosis. People who receive palliative care along with treatment for the cancer often have less severe symptoms, better quality of life, and report that they are more satisfied with treatment.

Palliative treatments and care vary widely and often include medication, nutritional changes, relaxation techniques, emotional and spiritual support, and other therapies. You may also receive palliative treatments similar to those meant to get rid of the cancer, such as chemotherapy, surgery, or radiation therapy. Palliative care should not be confused with hospice care, which is used when a cure is not likely or when people are in the last months of life.

Before treatment begins, talk with your doctor about the goals of each treatment in the treatment plan. You should also talk about the possible side effects of the specific treatment plan and palliative care options.

During treatment, your health care team may ask you to answer questions about your symptoms and side effects and to describe each problem. Be sure to tell the health care team if you are experiencing a problem. This helps the health care team treat any symptoms and side effects as quickly as possible. It can also help prevent more serious problems in the future.

Supportive care for people with pancreatic cancer may include:

Palliative chemotherapy

Any chemotherapy regimen discussed above may help relieve the symptoms of pancreatic cancer, such as lessening pain, improving a patient's energy and appetite, and stopping or slowing weight loss. This approach is used when the cancer has spread and cannot be cured, but the symptoms of the cancer can be improved with chemotherapy. When making decisions about palliative chemotherapy, it is important that you and your doctor weigh the benefits with the possible side effects and consider how each treatment might affect your quality of life.

Relieving bile duct or small intestine blockage

If the tumour is blocking the common bile duct or small intestine, placing a tiny tube called a stent can help keep the blocked area open. This procedure can be performed using nonsurgical approaches, such as ERCP, PTC, or endoscopy. A stent can be either plastic or metal. The type used depends on the availability, insurance coverage/cost, a person's expected lifespan, and whether the cancer will eventually be removed with surgery. In general, plastic stents are less expensive and are easier to insert and remove. However, they need to be replaced every few months, are associated with more infections, and are more likely to move out of place. Stents are typically placed inside the body, but sometimes, a tube may need to be placed through a hole in the skin of the abdomen to drain fluid, such as bile. This is called percutaneous drainage. Sometimes, a patient may need surgery to create a bypass, even if the tumour itself cannot be completely removed.

Improving digestion and appetite

A special diet, medications, and specially prescribed enzymes may help a person digest food better if their pancreas is not working well or has been partially or entirely removed. Meeting with a dietitian/nutritionist is recommended for most patients, especially for those who are losing weight and have a poor appetite because of the disease.

Controlling diabetes

Insulin will usually be recommended if a person develops diabetes due to the loss of insulin produced by the pancreas, which is more common after a total pancreatectomy.

Relieving pain and other side effects

Morphine-like drugs called opioid analgesics are often needed to help reduce pain. Special types of nerve blocks done by pain specialists may also be used. One type of nerve block is a celiac plexus block, which helps relieve abdominal or back pain. During a nerve block, the nerves are injected with either an anesthetic to stop pain for a short time or a medication that destroys the nerves and can relieve pain for a longer time. A nerve block can be performed either percutaneously (through the skin) or with an endoscopic ultrasound. Depending on where the tumour is located, radiation therapy can sometimes be used to relieve pain.

Recommended supportive care may also include complementary therapies, such as Budwig Protocol. It is important that you talk with your doctor before trying any complementary therapies to make sure they do not interfere with your other cancer treatments.

Palliative and supportive care is not limited to managing a patient's physical symptoms. There are also emotional issues, like anxiety and depression, and psychological issues that many patients experience and that can be managed with professional help and support. A professional can help with developing coping skills and the overall difficulty of dealing with cancer. Cancer also affects caregivers and loved ones, and they are encouraged to seek out support as well.

Om Verma

Alternative cancer treatments

We are fighting with cancer since the dawn of history. Every year we discover new diagnostic modalities, better radiotherapy techniques and lots of new chemotherapy drugs. But we have completely failed to defeat this disease called cancer. Think again, are we really going on the right path? Does conventional Medicine really targets upon the prime cause of cancer?

It's not that more effective alternative treatments for cancer don't exist − they most certainly do. It's just that the allopathic system isn't at all interested in divulging real cures. This is because their expensive therapies generate billions of dollars for the cancer industry.

Chemotherapy Doesn't Cure Cancer − It Causes It!

Chemotherapy does, in fact, kill cancer cells. But it also kills healthy cells, along with a patient's immune system and, really, anything else that crosses its path. At worst, such treatments kill patients more quickly than if they had chosen not to undergo them at all.

There's no money to be made in prescribing prevention advice like eating fewer chemicals and exercising more. The "bread and butter" of the cancer industry is unleashing the next, latest-and-greatest cancer drug. Not telling you how to avoid cancer in the first place.

Many people with cancer are interested in trying any treatment that may cure them safely, including complementary and alternative cancer treatments. There is growing evidence that these alternative cancer treatments give wonderful results. Here are some alternative cancer treatments that are very safe and effective.

63

- **Budwig Protocol** - The best Alternative Treatment effective in all cancers and all stages with documented 90% success

  - Laetrile (Vitamin B-17) Therapy

  - Gerson Therapy

  - Dr. Simoncini Baking Soda Cancer Treatment

  - High-dose vitamin C

  - Frankincense Essential Oil Therapy

  - Hyperthermia

  - Oxygen Therapy and Hyperbaric Chambers

Laetrile (Vitamin B-17) Therapy

Introduction

During 1950, after many years of research, a dedicated biochemist Dr. Ernest T. Krebs Jr., isolated a new vitamin from bitter apricot kernel that he called 'B-17' or 'Laetrile'. He conducted further lab animal and culture experiments to conclude that laetrile would be effective in the treatment of cancer. As the years rolled by, thousands became convinced that Krebs had finally found the treatment for all cancers. He proposed that cancer was caused by a deficiency of Vitamin B 17 (Laetrile, Amygdaline).

To prove that it was not toxic to humans he injected it into his own arm. As he predicted, there were no harmful or distressing side effects. The Laetrile had no harmful effect on normal cells but was deadly to cancer cells. Dr. Ernst Krebs stated that we need at least a minimum of 100 mg of B-17 or around 7 bitter apricot seeds to almost guarantee a cancer free life.

Nitriloside is a beta-cyanophoric glycosides, a large group of water-soluble, sugar-containing compounds found in a number of plants. Amygdalin is one of the most common nitrilosides. Laetrile is a partly man-made molecule and shares only part of the Amygdalin structure. Both Laetrile and Amygdalin have been promoted as "Vitamin B-17".

Laetrile stands for laevo-rotatory mandelonitrile beta-diglucoside. The "laevo" part references a purified form of B-17 that turns polarized light in a left-turning direction. Dr. Krebs, Jr. believed that only the left-rotating Laevo form was effective against cancer. So it's important to check the purity of your Laetrile.

65

How B-17 works (A tale of two enzymes)

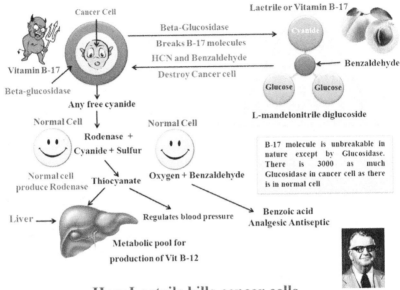

Cancer Cell

Laetrile or Vitamin B-17

Beta-Glucosidase
Breaks B-17 molecules
HCN and Benzaldehyde
Destroy Cancer cell

Cyanide

Benzaldehyde

Vitamin B-17

Glucose   Glucose

Beta-glucosidase

Any free cyanide

L-mandelonitrile diglucoside

Normal Cell   Normal Cell

Rodenase +
Cyanide + Sulfur

B-17 molecule is unbreakable in nature except by Glucosidase. There is 3000 as much Glucosidase in cancer cell as there is in normal cell

Normal cell
produce Rodenase   Thiocyanate   Oxygen + Benzaldehyde

Liver →   Regulates blood pressure

Benzoic acid
Analgesic Antiseptic

Metabolic pool for
production of Vit B-12

How Laetrile kills cencer cells

Dr. Om Verma   Dr. Ernst T. Krebs Jr

Laetrile, commonly known as Vitamin B-17 or Amygdalin, contains two units of Sugar, one of Benzaldehyde and one of Cyanide, all tightly locked within it. Everyone knows that cyanide can be highly toxic and even fatal if taken in sufficient quantity. However, as it is in locked state is completely inert and absolutely has no effect on living tissue. There is only one substance that can unlock this molecule and release the cyanide. That substance is an enzyme called beta-glucocidase, which we shall call the unlocking enzyme. When B-17 comes in contact with this enzyme, not only the cyanide is released but also Benzaldehyde which is highly toxic by itself. In fact, these two working together are at least 100 times more poisonous to cancer cell than either of them separately. The unlocking enzyme is not found to any dangerous degree anywhere in the body except at the cancer cell where it is present in great quantity. The result is that Vit B-17 is unlocked at the cancer cells becomes poisonous to the cancer cells and only to the cancer cells.

There is another important enzyme called Rodanese, which we shall identify as protecting enzyme. The reason is that it has the ability to neutralize cyanide by converting it instantly into the by-products (thiocyanate) that actually are beneficial and essential for health. This enzyme is found in great quantities in every part of the body except the cancer cells which consequently is not protected. Here then is a biochemical process that destroys cancer cells while at the same time nourishing and sustaining non-cancerous cells. It is intricate and perfect mechanism of nature that simply couldn't be accidental.

Laetrile - Metabolic Therapy

Metabolic therapy is a non-toxic cancer treatment based on the use of Vitamin B- 17, proteolytic pancreatic enzymes, immuno-stimulants, and vitamin and mineral supplements.

There are three parts to this program:

1. Laetrile

2. Vitamins and enzymes

3. Diet

Phase I Metabolic - Program for the first 21 days

Laetrile

Amygdalin (Laetrile) is available in 500 mg. tablets and in vials (10 cc 3 Gm) for intravenous use. Both forms are used. Two vials of Laetrile are given IV three times weekly for three weeks with at least one day between injections (Mon., Wed., Fri.). Dose of Amygdalin Tablets 500 mg is 2 tab three times a day with meals on the days on which the patients do not receive the intravenous Laetrile. Thiocyanate levels in the blood can be measured during treatment. In general, the patients who do best are those in whom the thiocyanate level is between 1.2 and 2.5 Mg/DL (Philip E.Binzel).

Vitamins and Enzymes

Preven-Ca Caps - Preven-Ca is a comprehensive blend of potent herb and fruit extracts, designed to provide a broad Spectrum of Flavonoids with scientifically demonstrated Antioxidant activity and effectiveness. One capsule with each meal.

Vitamin B15 - One capsule three times a daily at the end of each meal.

Megazyme Forte (Proteolytic Enzymes) Three tablets two hours after each meal (9 daily).

Ester Vitamin C 1000 mg capsule - One capsule with each meal.

Shark Cartilage It has been said that Sharks are the healthiest creature on earth. Sharks are immune to practically every disease known to man. One capsules three times a daily with each meal.

Natural Vitamin E 400 iu - One gel with lunch and one with dinner.

AHCC (Active Hexose Correlated Compound) - Two capsules with each meal.

Multi Vitamin & Mineral Liquid - 1 oz (two tablespoons) once daily with a meal.

Vitamin A & E Emulsion - 5 drops in juice or water three times per day.

Barley Grass Juice - One teaspoon in juice three times per day.

Bitter apricot seeds - No more than 12 every 2 hours 6 times a day.

Dimethyl sulfoxide (DMSO) - DMSO is a by-product of the wood and paper industry. It is known for its ability to permeate living tissue and stimulate cellular processes.

Or Phase 1 Oral

Injectable Amygdalin is replaced with 500mg Amygdalin tablets. Binzel recommends 2 of these tablets with each meal for a total of 6 per day. Otherwise the ORAL Phase 1 includes the same materials as above.

Phase 2 Metabolic - Program for the next 3 months

It comprises the same materials as Phase 1 except that the dosages for the vitamin B-17 as well as the A&E Emulsion Drops change to the following:

Vitamin B-17 500 mg tablets: 1 tablet with each meal and one at bedtime.

Vitamin A & E emulsion drops: 10 drops in juice or water two times per day (suspend for 2 months after 3 months of use).

Diet

Consume those fruits (i.e. seeds), grains and nuts that are rich in laetrile. Consume salads with healthy dressings. For protein patient should consume whole grains including corn, beans, buckwheat, nuts, dried fruits. Real butter in small amounts is permitted. The patients are not permitted anything which contains white flour or white sugar. Take away all meat, all poultry, all fish, all eggs and milk from patients. Margarine is detrimental to good nutrition. No coffee is permitted.

Zinc acts as transport vehicle for laetrile in the body. If patient does not have sufficient zinc, laetrile will not get into the tissues of the body. That's why you should give a spoonful of pumpkin seeds along with bitter apricot kernels. The body will not rebuild any tissue without sufficient quantities of Vitamin C etc.

Om Verma

The Gerson Therapy

The Gerson Therapy is a natural treatment that activates the body's extraordinary ability to heal itself through an organic, plant-based diet, raw juices, coffee enemas and natural supplements.

With its whole-body approach to healing, the Gerson Therapy naturally reactivates your body's magnificent ability to heal itself – with no damaging side effects. This a powerful, natural treatment boosts the body's own immune system to heal cancer, arthritis, heart disease, allergies, and many other degenerative diseases. Dr. Max Gerson developed the Gerson Therapy in the 1930s, initially as a treatment for his own debilitating migraines, and eventually as a treatment for degenerative diseases such as skin tuberculosis, diabetes and, most famously, cancer.

An abundance of nutrients from copious amounts of fresh, organic juices are consumed every day, providing your body with a super-dose of enzymes, minerals and nutrients. These substances then break down diseased tissue in the body, while coffee enemas aid in eliminating toxins from the liver.

Throughout our lives our bodies are being filled with a variety of carcinogens and toxic pollutants. These toxins reach us through the air we breathe, the food we eat, the medicines we take and the water we drink. The Gerson Therapy's intensive detoxification regimen eliminates these toxins from the body, so that true healing can begin.

How the Gerson Therapy Works

The Gerson Therapy regenerates the body to health, supporting each important metabolic requirement by flooding the body with nutrients from about 15- 20 pounds of organically-grown fruits and vegetables daily. Most is used to make fresh raw

71

juice, up to one glass every hour, up to 13 times per day. Raw and cooked solid foods are generously consumed. Oxygenation is usually more than doubled, as oxygen deficiency in the blood contributes to many degenerative diseases. The metabolism is also stimulated through the addition of thyroid, potassium and other supplements, and by avoiding heavy animal fats, excess protein, sodium and other toxins.

Degenerative diseases render the body increasingly unable to excrete waste materials adequately, commonly resulting in liver and kidney failure. The Gerson Therapy uses intensive detoxification to eliminate wastes, regenerate the liver, reactivate the immune system and restore the body's essential defences – enzyme, mineral and hormone systems. With generous, high-quality nutrition, increased oxygen availability, detoxification, and improved metabolism, the cells – and the body – can regenerate, become healthy and prevent future illness.

Juicing

Fresh-pressed juice from raw foods provides the easiest and most effective way of providing high-quality nutrition. By juicing, patients can take in the nutrients and enzymes from nearly 15 pounds of produce every day, in a manner that is easy to digest and absorb.

Every day, a typical patient on the Gerson Therapy for cancer consumes up to thirteen glasses of fresh, raw carrot-apple and green leaf juices. These juices are prepared hourly from fresh, raw, organic fruits and vegetables, using a two-step juicer or a masticating juicer used with a separate hydraulic press.

The Gerson Therapy Diet

The Gerson Therapy diet is plant-based and entirely organic. The diet is naturally high in vitamins, minerals, enzymes, micro-nutrients, and extremely low in sodium, fats, and proteins. The following is a typical daily diet for a Gerson patient on the full therapy regimen:

• Thirteen glasses of fresh, raw carrot-apple and green-leaf juices prepared hourly from fresh, organic fruits and vegetables.

• Three full plant-based meals, freshly prepared from organically grown fruits, vegetables and whole grains. A typical meal will include salad, cooked vegetables, baked potatoes, Hippocrates soup and juice.

• Fresh fruit and vegetables available at all hours for snacking, in addition to the regular diet.

Supplements

All medications used in connection with the Gerson Therapy are classed as biological, materials of organic origin that are supplied in therapeutic amounts. The supplements used on the Gerson Therapy include:

• Potassium compound

• Lugol's solution

• Vitamin B-12

• Thyroid hormone

• Pancreatic Enzymes

Detoxification

Coffee enemas are the primary method of detoxification of the tissues and blood on the Gerson Therapy. Coffee enemas accomplish this essential task, assisting the liver in eliminating toxic residues from the body for good. Cancer patients on the Gerson Therapy may take up to 5 coffee enemas per day. The Gerson Therapy also utilizes castor oil to stimulate bile flow and enhance the liver's ability to filter blood.

Om Verma

Simoncini's Soda bicarb Cancer Treatment

Dr. Tullio Simoncini is a medical doctor in Italy who has done more than anyone to explore the uses of the baking soda cancer treatment as an alternative cancer treatment. It is known that cancer creates and favours an acid environment and because of this, Dr. Simoncini and others have used sodium bicarbonate as an alkaline therapeutic agent.

The way that acidity seems to protect cancer is not fully understood. It seems that cytotoxic T-cells, which may attack cancer cells under normal conditions, are inactivated in an acid extracellular fluid. Also, the type of acidity that cancer produces, i.e., lactic acid, stimulates vascular endothelial growth factor and angiogenesis. This is like a highway project, which enables a tumour to build the blood vessels that it needs to bring the nutrients for it to survive. So the tumour creates an environment in which it can then exist comfortably.

Baking Soda's Alkalinity Fights Cancer's Acidity

At a pH of about 10, sodium bicarbonate is an antidote to this acidity. It can be used clinically in sterile, intravenous form. This is a liquid, sterile bicarbonate of soda. The baking soda cancer treatment is well-tolerated, even with frequent repeated dosing. Dr. Simonchini also injects soda bicarb solution directly into the tumours at his centre.

Cancer a Fungus problem?

Dr. Simonchini says that cancer is caused by fungus However; it is useful to know that not only does sodium bicarbonate disrupt the comfortable environment of tumours, but it also has anti-fungal effect.

Om Verma

Budwig Protocol
90% documented success in all types of Cancers

Bonding of Alpha-Linolenic Acid and Sulfurated Protein

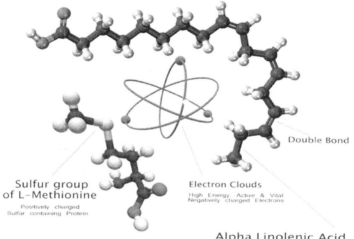

Sulfur group
of L-Methionine
Positively charged
Sulfur containing Protein

Electron Clouds
High Energy, Active & Vital
Negatively charged Electrons

Double Bond

Alpha Linolenic Acid

Dr. Budwig has been referred to as a top European cancer research scientist, biochemist, pharmacologist, and physicist. Dr. Budwig was a seven-time Nobel Prize nominee.

In Germany in 1952, she was the central government's senior expert for fats and pharmaceutical drugs. She's considered one of the world's leading authorities on fats and oils. Her research has shown the tremendous effects that commercially processed fats and oils (having Trans fatty acids) have in destroying cell membranes and lowering the voltage in the cells of our bodies, which then result in chronic and terminal disease including cancer.

What we have forgotten is that we are body electric. The cells of our body fire electrically. They have a nucleus in the centre of the cell which is positively charged, and the cell membrane, which is the outer lining of the cell, is negatively charged. We are all aware of how fats clog up our veins and arteries and are the leading cause of heart attacks, but we never looked beyond the end of our noses to see how these very dangerous fats and oils are affecting the overall health of our minds and bodies at the cellular level.

Dr. Budwig discovered that when unsaturated fats have been chemically treated, their unsaturated qualities are destroyed and the field of electrons removed. This commercial processing of fats destroys the field of electrons that the cell membranes (60-75 trillion cells) in our bodies must have to fire properly (i.e. function properly).

The fats' ability to associate with protein and thereby to achieve water solubility in the fluids of the living body is destroyed. As Budwig put it, "the battery is dead because the electrons in these fats and oils recharge it." When the electrons are destroyed the fats are no longer active and cannot flow into the capillaries and through the fine capillary networks. This is when circulation problems arise.

Without the proper metabolism of fats in our bodies, every vital function and every organ is affected. This includes the generation of new life and new cells. Our bodies produce over 500 million new cells daily. Dr. Budwig points out that in growing new cells, there is a polarity between the electrically positive nucleus and the electrically negative cell membrane with its high unsaturated fatty acids. During cell division, the cell, and new daughter cell must contain enough electron-rich fatty acids in the cell's surface area to divide off completely from the old cell. When this process is interrupted the body begins to die. In essence, these commercially processed fats and oils are shutting down the electrical field of the cells allowing chronic and terminal diseases to take hold of our bodies.

A very good example would be tumours. Dr. Budwig noted that "The formation of tumours usually happens as follows. In those body areas which normally host many growth processes, such as in the skin and membranes, the glandular organs, for example, the liver and pancreas or the glands in the stomach and intestinal tract—it is here that the growth processes are brought to a standstill. Because the polarity is missing, due to the lack of electron rich highly unsaturated fat, the course of growth is disturbed—the surface-active fats are not present; the substance becomes inactive before the maturing and shedding process of the cells ever takes place, which results in the formation of tumours."

She pointed out that this can be reversed by providing the simple foods, cottage cheese, and flax seed oil, which revises the stagnated growth processes. This naturally causes the tumour or tumours present to dissolve and the whole range of symptoms which indicate a "dead battery are cured." Dr. Budwig did not believe in the use of growth-inhibiting treatments such as chemotherapy or radiation. She was quoted as saying "I flat declare that the usual hospital treatments today, in a case of tumorous growth, most certainly leads to worsening of the disease or a speedier death, and in healthy people, quickly causes cancer."

Dr. Budwig discovered that when she combined flaxseed oil, with its powerful healing nature of essential electron rich unsaturated fats, and cottage cheese, which is rich in sulfur protein, the bonding produced makes the oil water soluble and easily absorbed into the cell membrane.

I found testimonials of people from around the world who had been diagnosed with terminal cancer (all types of cancer), sent home to die and were now living healthy, normal lives. Not only had Dr. Budwig been using her protocol for treating cancer in Europe, but she also treated other chronic diseases such as arthritis, heart infarction, irregular heartbeat, psoriasis, eczema (other skin diseases), immune deficiency syndromes (Multiple Sclerosis and other autoimmune diseases), diabetes, lungs (respiratory conditions), stomach ulcers, liver, prostate, strokes, brain tumours, brain (strengthens activity), arteriosclerosis and other chronic diseases. Dr. Budwig's protocol proved successful where orthodox traditional medicine was failing.

Om Verma

Otto Warburg – Biography

Dr. Otto Warburg (Oct 8, 1883 Aug 1, 1970)

Otto Heinrich Warburg (October 8, 1883 – August 1, 1970), son of physicist Emil Warburg, was a German physiologist, medical doctor and Nobel laureate. His mother was the daughter of a Protestant family of bankers and civil servants from Baden. Warburg studied chemistry under the great Emil Fischer, and earned his "Doctor of Chemistry" in Berlin in 1906. He then earned the degree of "Doctor of Medicine" in Heidelberg in 1911. Between 1908 and 1914, Warburg was affiliated with the Naples Marine Biological Station, in Naples, Italy, where he conducted research.

He served as an officer in the elite Uhlan (cavalry regiment) during the First World War, and was given the Iron Cross (1st Class) award for his bravery. Warburg is considered one of the 20th century's leading biochemists. Towards the end of the war, Albert Einstein, who had been a friend of Warburg's father Emil, wrote Warburg asking him to leave the army and return to academia, since it would be a tragedy for the world to lose his talents. Einstein and Warburg later became friends, and Einstein's work in physics had great influence on Otto's biochemical research.

While working at the Marine Biological Station, Warburg performed research on oxygen consumption in sea urchin eggs after fertilization, and proved that upon fertilization, the rate of respiration increases by as much as six fold. His experiments also proved that iron is essential for the development of the larval stage.

In 1918, Warburg was appointed professor at the Kaiser Wilhelm Institute for Biology in Berlin-Dahlem. By 1931 he was promoted as director of the Kaiser Wilhelm Institute for Cell Physiology, which was later on, renamed the Max Planck Society. Warburg investigated the metabolism of tumours and the respiration of cells, particularly cancer cells, and in 1931 was awarded the Nobel Prize in Physiology for his "discovery of the nature and mode of action of the respiratory enzyme."

Nomination for a second Nobel Prize

In 1944, Warburg was nominated for a second Nobel Prize in Physiology by Albert Szent-Györgyi, for his work on nicotinamide, the mechanism and enzymes involved in fermentation, and the discovery of flavin (in yellow enzymes), but was prevented from receiving it by Adolf Hitler's regime.

Otto Warburg edited and had much of his original work published in The Metabolism of Tumours and wrote New Methods of Cell Physiology (1962). Otto Warburg was thrilled when Oxford University awarded him an honorary doctorate.

In his later years, Warburg was convinced that illness is resulted from pollution; this caused him to become a bit of a health advocate. He insisted on eating bread made from wheat grown organically on his farm. When he visited restaurants, he often made arrangements to pay the full price for a cup of tea, but to only be served boiling water, from which he would make tea with a tea bag he had brought with him. He was also known to go to significant lengths to obtain organic butter, the quality of which he trusted.

The Otto Warburg Medal

The Otto Warburg Medal is intended to commemorate Warburg's outstanding achievements. It has been awarded by the German Society for Biochemistry and Molecular Biology since 1963. The prize honours and encourages pioneering achievements in fundamental biochemical and molecular biological research. The Otto Warburg Medal is regarded as the highest award for biochemists and molecular biologists in Germany.

Prime cause of Cancer

Warburg hypothesized that cancer growth is caused by tumour cells mainly generating energy (as e.g. adenosine triphosphate / ATP) by anaerobic breakdown of glucose (known as fermentation, or anaerobic respiration). This is in contrast to healthy cells, which mainly generate energy from oxidative breakdown of pyruvate. Pyruvate is an end product of glycolysis, and is oxidized within the mitochondria. Hence, and according to Warburg, cancer should be interpreted as a mitochondrial dysfunction.

In short, Warburg summarized that all normal cells absolutely require oxygen, but cancer cells can live without oxygen - a rule without exception. Deprive a cell 35% of its oxygen for 48 hours and it would become cancerous. Dr. Otto Warburg clearly mentioned that the root cause of cancer is lack of oxygen in the cells.

He also discovered that cancer cells are anaerobic (do not breathe oxygen), get the energy by fermenting glucose and produce levo-rotating lactic acid, and the body becomes acidic. Cancer cannot survive in the presence of high levels of oxygen, as found in an alkaline state.

He postulated that sulfur containing protein and some unknown fat is required to attract oxygen into the cell. This fat plays a major role in the respiration and functioning of Warburg respiratory enzyme. He thought it would be butyric acid and made experiment, but this attempt was a failure. For many decades scientists were trying to identify this unknown and mysterious fat but nobody succeeded (Otto Warburg, Wikipedia).

Om Verma

Dr. Johanna Budwig - Biography and Science

Birth of an angel

A lovely couple, Hermann Budwig and Elisabeth, lived in Essen town of Germany situated on the bank of river Ruhr. On the eve of 30th September, 1908 Elisabeth delivered a brilliant and lucky angel. Hermann and Elisabeth were very happy, and celebrating. They called her Johanna. In German, Johanna means a gift from God. In the family and neighbourhood everybody was talking that Johanna is very lucky, she will study in a college and  become a big doctor. Actually, 1908 was very fortunate and important year for the freedom of women in Germany. Government for the first time in history, changed laws, and allowed women to study in college and Universities. Also the German parliament passed a legislation to allow women to become members of political parties and prestigious clubs. Though women were given new rights and freedom, liberalization was slow and old values still persisted.

The tough life of a sage of science

Unluckily, Elisabeth died in 1920; family members thought that her father, being a poor loco mechanic, might not look after Johanna. So she was sent to an orphanage. This was a great shock for the little Johanna, but it had one positive side also. Education up to higher level was totally free for orphans.

In 1926, Germany was slowly recovering from the after effects of the First World War. Economic conditions were improving. Scholars and scientists were developing new technologies in every field. One third of all Nobel Prizes were being given to German academics.

Deaconess at Kaiserswerth

Johanna was very intelligent and sharp in studies from the beginning. In order to achieve good future, she decided to join the renowned Deaconess's Institute   of Kaiserswerth in 1925. Theodor Fliedner, a pastor, founded Kaiserswerth Institute for welfare of unmarried mothers, prisoners, patients, orphans and poor children in 1836. In the beginning a Hospital and a Nursing School was established. This school was very famous Nursing School of that time. Florence Nightingale, known as mother of modern nursing, also studied in this Deaconess School in 1850. Intelligent Johanna easily got admission in this Institute. She was made a "deaconess" on March 30, 1932. This was the most appropriate place for her. There was a 1000 bedded hospital, pharmacy and a boarding school.   She decided to study pharmacy.

After completing preliminary education in Kaiserswerth, she joined Münster University for further studies. Her analytical thinking and precise knowledge was noticed by her Professor Dr Hans Paul Kaufmann. He always encouraged and helped her. Here she passed state examination in pharmacy and was rewarded distinction in chemistry in 1936. Then she continued further education in physics, and received the title "Doctor of Science" at the University of Münster in 1938. On August 1, 1939, she was appointed as in-charge of pharmacy at the Military Hospital in Kaiserswerth.

Next month, Hitler's military forces attacked Poland. During war time, brave Johanna was busy in organizing and expanding the pharmacy. The war was not an easy time. There were two thousand people living in Kaiserswerth. Johanna was responsible for ensuring that there were enough medicines in this time of rationing and a thriving black market. She was well prepared and ready to fulfil any emergency demand for her patients. Many of her fellow deaconesses were often jealous and not co-operating but she continued evolving her professional skills. She was strong and was confronting every opponent (Dr. Johanna Budwig Stiftung).

Dr Budwig's scientific thinking, work and career

After Second World War, Johanna left Kaiserswerth in 1949. Soon Prof. Kaufmann came to know that she had left Kaiserswerth. He immediately met and persuaded her to work with him in Münster University, as he was always impressed from her talent. He converted the basement of his house into a laboratory and arranged all facilities for her research. He was famous as Fat Pope in the whole Europe.

On Prof. Kaufmann's recommendation, Johanna was appointed as the chief expert for drugs and fats at the Federal Institute for Fats Research, Germany. This was the country's largest office issuing the approval of new drugs used for cancer. Many applications had been submitted to her for approval. These were the medications for cancer therapy with the sulfhydryl group (sulfur-containing protein compounds). Everywhere she saw that fats played a role in cellular respiration, also in expert reports provided by well-known professors like Prof. Nonnenbruch. Unfortunately, fats could only be detected in the late stage, and there were no method to distinguish between fats chemically.

By this time, she developed paper chromatography. With this technique for first time she was able to detect fatty acids and lipoproteins directly even in 0.1 ml of blood. She used Co60 isotopes successfully to produce the first differential reaction for fatty acids, and produced the first direct iodine value via radioiodine. She also developed control of atmosphere in a closed system by using gas systems which act as antioxidants. She further developed Coloring methods, separating effects of fats and fatty acids. She too studied their behaviour in blue and red light with fluorescent dyes.

Using rhodamine red dye, she studied the electrical behaviour of the unsaturated fatty acids with their "halo". With this technique she could prove that electron rich highly unsaturated Linoleic and Linolenic fatty acids (Flax oil being the richest source) were  the mysterious and undiscovered decisive fats required to attract oxygen into the cells, which Otto Warburg could not find. She studied the electromagnetic function of pi-electrons of the linolenic acid in the cell membranes, for nerve function, secretions, mitosis, as well as cell division. She also examined the synergism of the sulfur containing protein with the pi-electrons of the highly unsaturated fatty acids and their significance for the formation of the hydrogen bridge between fat and protein, which represent "the only path" for fast and focused Transport of electrons during respiration. This research was extensively published in 1950 in Neue Wege in der Fettforschung (New Directions in Fat Research) and other publications.

This immediately caused an excitement and turmoil in the scientific community. Everybody thought that it would open new doors in Cancer research. She also proved that hydrogenated fats and refined oils including all Trans-fatty acids were not having vital electrons and were respiratory poisons.

During her research, she found that the blood of seriously ill cancer patients had deficiency of unsaturated essential fats (Linoleic and Linolenic fatty acids), lipoproteins, phosphatides, and hemoglobin. She also had noticed that cancer patients had a strange greenish-yellow substance in their blood which is not present in the blood of healthy people (Budwig, Cancer The Problem And The Solution).

She wanted to develop a healing program for cancer. So she enrolled over 642 cancer patients from four hospitals in Münster. She gave Flax oil and Cottage Cheese to these patients. After just three months, patients began to improve in health and strength, the yellow green substance in their blood began to disappear, tumours gradually receded and at the same time the nutrients began to rise.

This way she developed a simple cure for cancer, based on the consumption of Flax oil with low fat Quark or cottage cheese, raw organic diet, mild exercise, Flax oil massage and the healing powers of the sun. It was a great victory and the first milestone in the battle against cancer. She treated approx. 2500 cancer patients during last few decades. Prof. Halme of surgery clinic in Helsinki used to keep records of her patients. According to him her success was over 90%, and this was achieved in cases, which were rejected by Allopathic doctors.

Dr. Budwig was a courageous scientist. She loudly and convincingly argued that consumption of highly processed foods, particularly edible oils and margarines, which block the oxidation processes in the cells, are responsible for the development of cancer and other degenerative diseases. She met with great resistance from food industry giants, who were doing everything to prevent the spread of her sensational discovery. In 1952, under the influence of strong pressure from this lobby, she lost her job and was barred from the research work.

Joins Medical School at Göttingen

Opponents of Dr. Johanna blamed her that she should not treat cancer patients because she doesn't have a doctor's degree. She felt this and eventually joined medical school in Göttingen in 1955. Budwig was 47 years old at that time. She also continued her research work along with her studies. Budwig successfully treated Prof. Martius's wife, who suffered from Breast Cancer

One night a woman came with her small child whose arm was supposed to be amputated due to a tumour. She treated her and soon the amputation surgery was dismissed, and the child quickly did very well.

A Swiss woman came to her clinic in Göttingen. She suffered from Colon Cancer with metastasis and intestinal obstruction. Several doctors examined her, and were to be operated on Christmas Eve. On Budwig's request, she was treated by her protocol. The tumour of the colon quickly subsided. Seven weeks later, she was discharged without any detectable tumour. It is interesting that the Swiss custom officer was not ready to believe that the submitted passport belonged to same lady. Her look was so much changed! At home her daughter welcomed saying: "You look healthy, younger and more beautiful (from her book The Death of the Tumour – Vol. II).

After this, University allowed her to treat cancer patients with her oil-protein diet. She was getting miraculous results. University professors were excited with the results, but wanted that she should also include chemo and radiotherapy. She was rigid and didn't want to compromise. So she had differences and conflicts with her professors and ultimately left Göttingen (Budwig, Cancer The Problem And The Solution).

Last Destination - Dietersweiler-Freudenstadt

Eventually, she shifted to Dietersweiler-Freudenstadt, where she lived till her death. There she completed Ph.D. in Naturopathy so that she could legally treat cancer patients. She continued treating her patients in Freudenstadt. In 1968 she created unique Eldi oils for massage and enema, called Electron

Differential Oils after performing precise spectroscopic measurements of the light absorption in different oils. US pain institute has written somewhere: "What this crazy woman does with her ELDI oils, none of us manages to do via pain killers."

Budwig conducted more than 200 lectures worldwide. Dr. Budwig was popular in the U.S. as FLAX SEED lady from Freudenstadt. She delivered her last public Lecture in Freudenstadt on March 3, 1999. On November 28, 2002, she fell down in her bathroom and got a fracture in right femur neck. She was admitted in a nursing home and ultimately died on May 19, 2003.

Om Verma

Budwig Protocol

The Budwig Protocol is one of the most widely followed alternative treatments for cancer and other diseases. The diet seems simple, but foods are powerful and can heal a person.

Transition Diet

The Transition diet is especially recommended for patients of liver, pancreatic or gall bladder cancers. The basic principle is that for 3 days nothing is eaten and drunk except the following written and at least three times daily warm tea (herbal teas from peppermint, rose hip, mallow or green tea) is drunk. Dr Budwig has recommended variant 1 for patients with a relatively good energy state, and variant 2 and 3 mainly for seriously ill patients.

Variant 1

Variant 1 for three days, 250 g of linomel or alternatively freshly crushed Flax seed is eaten together with the following:

- Freshly pressed fruit juices without added sugar.

- Freshly pressed vegetable juices such as carrot, celery juice, red beetroots and apple juice.

- Chinese tea and black tea are allowed in the morning

- Honey for sweetening is allowed. Just as grape juice for drinking and as a sweetener. Energetically weak patients can also consume sparkling wine and linomel.

Variant 2

For three days, oat meal cereal very hour with linomel is eaten daily with the following juices:

- Freshly pressed fruit juices or freshly pressed vegetable juices such as carrot, celery juice, beetroot and apple juice.

- Chinese tea and black tea are allowed in the morning.

93

• Honey for sweetening is allowed. Just as grape juice for drinking and as a sweetener.

• Energetically weak patients can also consume sparkling wine and linomel.

Variant 3

For three days, oatmeal soup with linomel is given three times a day together with the following juices:

• Freshly pressed fruit juices or fruit juices without added sugar.

• Freshly pressed vegetable juices such as carrot, celery juice, beetroot and apple juice.

• Chinese tea and black tea are allowed in the morning.

• Honey for sweetening is allowed. Just as grape juice for drinking and as a sweetener.

Energetically weak patients can also consume sparkling wine and linomel.

It is often experienced frequently that patients mixed all three variants and "nevertheless" had good results. So better you to stick to one variant. (Budwig – Cancer The Problem And The Solution 2005: p.36).

Budwig Diet

The Budwig Protocol is necessary for many diseases from cancer to type 2 diabetes and heart disease to autoimmune diseases, etc. Its purpose is to energize the cells by restoring the natural electrical potential in the cell. Many human diseases are caused by "sick cells" which have lost their normal electrical potential; generally via a lower ATP energy in the cell's mitochondria.

6:00 AM – Sauerkraut juice

A glass of sauerkraut juice consumed before breakfast every morning. It is rich in vitamins including C, enzymes and helps develop the health-promoting gut flora. Sauerkraut is cabbage that has been pickled by natural fermentation, mainly with lactobacillus bacteria. It is slightly salty, sharp and sour. Well made, it is much nicer than it sounds. You may also consume another glass of sauerkraut juice later in the day.

It interesting that sauerkraut contains right rotating lactic acids and is highly alkaline and neutralizes levo-rotating lactic acids and makes our body alkaline. That is why Marcus Porcius Cato the Elder issued a statement - Carcinomas are incurable except with the treatment with Sauerkraut.

8:00 AM Breakfast
Green or herbal tea

Start breakfast with a cup of warm herbal or green tea. Sweeten with only natural honey. You can add lemon or grape juice. Patient should take such a tea before or with Linomel Muesli. You may consume 4-5 such teas in a day.

Linomel Muesli or Oil-Protein Muesli

This should be made fresh and consumed within 15 minutes. It is full of high energy pi-electrons, attract oxygen in the cells and capable of healing cell membranes. It is full of energy-rich

omega-3 fats, has power to attract healing photons from sun through resonance. As "Om" is divine word and synonym of God in India. According to Hindu Mythology, the whole universe is located inside "Om", so the name Omkhand has been given to this wonderful recipe in Hindi.

Ingredients

- 3 Tbsp cold pressed organic Flax seed oil (FO)
- 100-125gm (6 Tbsp) Quark or Cottage Cheese(CC)
- 2 Tbsp freshly ground Flax seeds
- 2 Tbsp milk
- 1 cup fruits
- ¼ cup dried nuts
- Natural honey
- Flavourings – lemon, apple cider vinegar, cinnamon, pure cacao, natural vanilla, shredded coconut etc.

Recipe

Place 2 tablespoons Linomel or freshly ground Flax seeds in a small bowl. It is covered with raw, crushed or diced seasonal fruits depending on the season. Pour some orange or grape juice over this. Linomel^{Tm} is a brand name and originally created and patented by Budwig. It is a cereal made

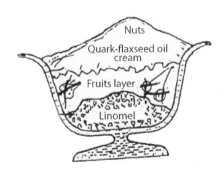

from cracked Flax Seed, a small amount of honey and a little milk powder.

Then the Quark-Flax seed oil cream is prepared in as follows: First add Flax seed oil, milk and honey and blend briefly with a hand-held immersion electric blender, then gradually add the Quark in smaller portions. Blend till oil and Quark is thoroughly mixed with no separated oil. Then it is seasoned differently everyday with different flavourings such as vanilla, cinnamon or various fruits such as banana, apple, lemon, orange juice, or berries.

Use various fruits such as fresh berries, apple, cherry, orange, banana, papaya, grapes etc. Add other fresh fruit if you like, totalling ½ to 1 cup of fruit. Budwig specially advised to use berries like strawberry, blueberry, raspberry, cheery etc. because berries have ellagic acids which are strong cancer fighters.

Add organic raw nuts such as walnuts, almonds, raisins or Brazil nuts. They have sulfurated proteins, omega-3 fats and vitamins. Brazil nut is especially important because a single nut provides you with all of the selenium you need for the day. Selenium is very important to boost immune power. Peanuts are prohibited.

For variety and flavour, try natural vanilla, cinnamon, lemon juice, pure cocoa or shredded coconut.

Once blended in Budwig Cream, Quark and Flax seed oil form a new substance called lipoprotein. Lipoprotein is a water soluble complex. The Quark is rich in the sulfur-containing amino acids, methionine and cysteine. These positively charged amino acids attract the negatively charged electron clouds in fatty acid chains and exhibit a stabilizing effect on the highly unsaturated, otherwise easily oxidized fats. Thus, the amino acids protect the polyunsaturated fatty acids from the Flax seed oil against oxidation which, as a result, are able to enter the human body unchanged and with their full energy potential. The result: they are much more valuable to cells and their membranes.

Consequently, one could say that Quark excels as a protector for the polyunsaturated fatty acids.

Sulfur-rich amino acids play a wealth of roles in many vital functions in our bodies. In combination with polyunsaturated fatty acids, they are important partners in regulating the uptake of oxygen and its utilization by the cell. They therefore contribute significantly to a strong immune system, healthy metabolism, and mental vitality. For many generations, people have been getting their omega-3 fatty acids from fish, vegetables, nuts, and seeds. Our health literally depends on the regular consumption of the essential omega-3 and omega-6 fatty acids, alpha-linolenic acid (ALA) and linoleic acid (LA). Our bodies require these fatty acids in order to synthesize their cell membranes as well as for a variety of metabolic processes and heal the cancer and other diseases.

Tips for making the Budwig Mixture

- Follow directions properly! It is important to add things to the mixture in the right order. If you mix them in the wrong order you may lose a lot of the opportunity to convert the oil-soluble omega-3 into water soluble-omega-3.

- Keep the Flax seed oil refrigerated.

- Immersion blender is a must.

- The mixture can be flavoured differently every day by adding nuts and fruits preferably organic such as pecans, almonds or walnuts (not peanuts), banana, organic cocoa, shredded coconut, pineapple (fresh) blueberries, raspberries, cinnamon, vanilla or (freshly) squeezed fruit juice.

- Consume immediately for best results.

10 AM Vegetable juice

Freshly squeezed vegetable juice from carrots, beets, celery, tomato, and radish, lemon as well as green vegetables - stinging nettle, lettuce or spinach. Apple is added to sweeten and enhance the taste. Carrot & beet juices are especially helpful to the liver and have strong cancer fighting properties. Vary vegetables. Some tasty and nutritious combinations are beet and apple juice, carrot and apple, carrot and beet, asparagus and apple, celery and apple, celery and carrot. Beet juice should not be taken alone. If taken alone it may cause red or pink urine (beeturia).

She also frequently recommended the following juices:

1. Nettle juice - Especially in the spring, Dr Budwig recommended to puree nettles with water and a lemon.

2. Radish juice - For this, a radish is first crushed and then thrown together with a lemon into the juicer. This juice is by the way durable for several days and Dr Budwig has sometimes recommended her patients to drink a small quantity of them every day.

3. Coltsfoot juice - For this juice, with the exception of the harder old rootstock, the entire remaining underground shoot is mixed with a few flowers and some milk and honey.

4. Horseradish juice - Mix 3-5 cm horseradish together with an apple and (raw) milk. Depending on the quantity of milk you can change the taste. Dr Budwig recommended this juice above all to workmen and to stimulate the appetite. Freshly pressed means, by the way, that you drink the juice within 5 minutes after pressing. In some cases, Dr Budwig prescribed a second juice 30 to 60 minutes later.

12:15 PM Lunch

Salad Platter: Salad plate with homemade cottage cheese-Flax seed mayonnaise. As salad also use: dandelion, cress, celery, tomato, cucumber, lettuce, radish, cabbage, broccoli, green horseradish and pepper.

Delicious mayo salad dressing can be prepared by mixing together 2 Tbsp (30 ml) Flax Oil, 2 Tbsp (30 ml) milk, and 2 Tbsp (30 ml) cottage cheese. Then add 2 tablespoons (30 ml) of Lemon juice (or Apple Cider Vinegar) and add 1 teaspoon (2.5 g) Mustard powder plus some herbs of your choice. Other alternative dressing can be made by mixing Flax Oil, lemon juice, Mustard and some herbs (Budwig, The Oil-Protein Diet Cookbook, 1994).

Main Course: Vegetables cooked in water, then flavoured with Oleolox and herbs possibly with oatmeal, soy sauce, curry etc. Vegetable broth flavoured with a little Oleolox and yeast flakes. As side dish for the vegetables: buckwheat, brown rice, millet or potatoes can be used. One or two slices of Ezekiel bread can be taken. Use lot of dried fruits in the main meal also.

Lunch Dessert: Cottage cheese/ Flax oil mixture served as a dessert, prepared with dry fruits and fruits such as apple, or poured over a fruit salad. You already know how to prepare it perfectly. You will find wonderful recipes for a delicious dessert in the Oil-Protein cookbook by Budwig. Please note that the dessert is "a must" and should definitely be eaten. So keep your main course light so you may enjoy the dessert happily.

The form of preparation as "fruit foam," "Linovita" or "red coat in the snow" (in Oil-Protein cookbook) is always welcoming for the healthy and the sick. In all the gimmicks in the preparation of the delicious desserts, one should be aware: Quark and Flaxseed give the patient immense power within a short space of time. Always fresh and beautiful, always freshly

interesting, this important food for life should be for the sick and for the whole family.

3 PM Fruit juices

In the afternoon, Dr Budwig recommended different kinds of fruit juices e.g. apples, grapes, cherries, pineapples, papaya, or apricot, sparkling wine or wine - with or without Flaxseeds or with or without a few drops Flaxseed oil.

Budwig preferred papaya juice and recommended her patients to drink at least every 2 days a glass of papaya juice. The main reason for this was definitely the protein splitting enzyme papain.

6 PM Dinner

The evening meal should be light and served early, around 6 p.m. A warm meal may be prepared using brown rice, buckwheat or oat meal. Never consume corn or soy beans. Dishes made with buckwheat grouts are most easily tolerated and nourishing. Use only honey to sweeten. Soup or more solid dishes can be combined with a tasty sauce according to preference. Use OLEOLOX liberally also to  sweet sauces and soups, making them nourishing and a richer source of energy.

8:30 PM

A glass of organic red wine may be consumed. All things are a matter of correct dosage. This glass of red wine is not a "must" program. In fact, seriously ill patients having pain and discomfort just starting on the oil-protein diet, it is recommended to serve a glass of red wine mixed with freshly ground Flax seeds to tide them over while going off pain killers (Budwig, Cancer The Problem And The Solution).

METRIC CONVERSION TABLE	
10 g = 0.35 oz	5 cc = 1 teaspoon
100 g = 3.5 oz	15 cc = 1 tablespoon
150 g = 5.25 oz	30 cc = 1 ounce
250 g = 8.8 oz	250 cc = 1 cup
454 g = 1 lb	960 cc = 1 qt
Oz = ounce lb = pound qt = quart Tsp = teaspoon Tbsp = tablespoon	

Precautions

Drink filtered water - Use RO (Reverse Osmosis)water for drinking, cooking and enemas.

Eat Organic Diet - Always try to eat organic food.

Dental Care –

Mercury is a Carcinogenic as well as a Poison! The root canals of dead teeth are full of bacteria that attack the liver and lymphatic system. From Amalgam fillings the mercury slowly leaks out of the filings. The ADA cleverly defends the use of amalgam in spite of the fact that there is sufficient evidence that patients with many severe problems, including psychotic episodes and fatal allergic reactions, were just cured by removing the amalgam. It is advisable to rather have a ceramic filling than be slowly poisoned by mercury. Even gold filling is dangerous; it acts as battery producing electrical current. Be informed that the effect of drugs, including poison, is dose dependant and cumulative.

Fluoride is not only toxic but it is also carcinogenic. Fluoride has never been proven to prevent tooth decay. It has been outlawed in many countries or groups of countries because the evidence is overwhelming that fluoride causes premature aging, so drink bottled water and use fluoride-free toothpaste (American Cancer Institute - 1963).

I highly recommend helping you avoid fillings in the first place. Holistic dentist recommend 3% H202 as a gargle or rinse, or making a paste using baking soda. H202 usage three times a day is advised. It is great for cleaning dentures, too.

Frying and deep frying - Frying and deep frying is not allowed to cook patient's food. Never heat any oil in the kitchen. By heating oil's the wealth of high energy electrons is destroyed and Tran's fats and dangerous toxic chemicals such as acrylamides are formed in the oil. Boiling and steaming are good practices. You can fry vegetables etc. in water and add oleolox before serving. Water is the safest medium for frying, says Lothar Hirneise.

Chemo and Radiotherapy - Chemotherapy is aimed at destruction of the tumour, and it destroys many living cells, and the entire person. Anything that disturbs growth is fatal because growth is an elementary function of life. We cannot achieve something good with bad tools.

Budwig rejects Chemo and Radiation Therapy. Budwig used to say with full confidence and clarity, "My treatment targets on the real cause of cancer; it fills cancer cells with

103

high energy pi-electrons and attracts oxygen into the cells. And cancer cells start to breathe and produce vital energy."

Man-made Supplements - With this treatment man-made antioxidants, synthetic vitamins and pain killers should not be given. The dose of anticoagulants and aspirin should be adjusted by your doctor. Dr. Budwig favours natural, herbal and homeopathy instead of man-made and synthetic supplements, vitamins and pain killers (Budwig, Cancer The Problem And The Solution).

Prohibitions of Budwig Protocol

In this protocol there are certain restrictions. They are as important as the diet itself. It is very difficult to defeat the cancer without strictly following these rules.

Sugar is strictly forbidden

Sugar, Jiggery, molasses, maple syrup and artificial sweeteners like xylitol, aspartame are not permitted. You can use only natural honey, stevia and fruit juices – all off course unprocessed.

Avoid meats, eggs and fish

Meat, fish, poultry, eggs, and butter are never allowed. Preserved meat is like a poison. It is highly processed and treated with dangerous antibiotics, preservatives and nitrates.

Stop using Hydrogenated Fat and Refined oil

You can never eat pizza, burger, fast food, fried food, biscuits etc. as they all are made by hydrogenated margarine and shortenings. Hydrogenation is a very dangerous process, used to increase shelf life of fats. In this process (oil is heated at very high temperature and hydrogen is passed through oils in presence of nickel) killing Trans fats are formed, high energy live and vital electrons are destroyed and nutrients are damaged. Hydrogenated Fats is just a dead, nutrition-less and cancer causing liquid plastic. Budwig always preached against these damaging fats. She has allowed low fat cheese, oleolox and coconut oil.

Preservatives and Processed Food

You should not eat Potato chips, soft drinks etc. which are full of preservatives. Never consume highly processed food e.g. ready to eat packed foods, pasta, pastries, bread and soy products, tofu etc. However good quality soy souse is permitted.'

Microwave, Teflon, Aluminium and Plastic

Never cook in microwave oven. Food cooked in microwave become toxic and deformed. Also don't use aluminium, plastic, Teflon coated cookware and aluminium foils. Use stainless steel, iron, china clay or glass utensils instead.

Chemicals and pesticides

Avoid pesticides and chemicals, even those in household products & cosmetics. Stay away from mosquito repellents, sun screen lotions and sun glasses.

Wear natural fibbers

Don't wear clothes made using synthetic fibber like nylon, polyester and acrylic. Budwig put great emphasis on the fact that her patients only wore natural fabrics such as cotton or satin, since they too can influence the magnetic field of our body.

Bed

Don't use on foam pillow and mattress. She recommended horsehair mattresses. Latex mattresses are the second choice. In any case, however, you should always replace mattresses that have metal spring cores.

CRT TV and mobile phones

These emit dangerous electromagnetic radiation, so do not use them. You can watch LCD and plasma TVs.

No left over

Food should be prepared fresh and eaten soon after preparation to maximize intake of health giving electrons and enzymes (Budwig, Cancer The Problem And The Solution).

Few Desserts recipes by Budwig

Fujiya delight

Ingredients for 3 people:

- 250 cc grape juice, 250 cc pure currant juice,

- 8g agar-agar, Quark-Flaxseed oil,

- Milk, honey, vanilla cream

Preparation:

Heat the grape juice till it boils, then add the currant juice, agar-agar, stirring constantly for 5 minutes, and allow to cool. Now divide this mass to 3 narrow, tall cups, which have been rinsed with cold water. It is preferable if these cups have a bottom diameter of only 3- 4 cm. Refrigerate to cool. Now mix a Quark-Flaxseed oil cream with milk, honey and vanilla. Turn the red jelly upside down onto glass plates. The Quark-Flaxseed oil cream is placed on the top so that only the upper half is covered with the Quark-Flaxseed oil cream, so that top looks like the Snow caped Mount Fujiyama.

(The beautiful hotel with a gorgeous view of the Fujiyama is called "Fujiya", hence the dessert "Fujiya".)

Linovita-in-love in wine jelly

Ingredients: for 5 people:

- 250 cc of grape juice, 250 ccm of white wine,

- 8 agar-agar, 4 tablespoons of milk,

- 8 tablespoons of Flaxseed oil, 2 teaspoons of honey,

- 200-250 g of Quark, 2 liqueur glasses

- Vodka, plum (Slibowitz) or cherry brandy or rum

Preparation:

The wine jelly is prepared by heating 250 cc of grape juice till it boils. Agar-agar is stirred with a little wine and placed in the boiling grape juice. Immediately remove from the cooking plate and add the remaining wine gradually with constant stirring. After about 5 minutes, the jelly mixture clears itself. You can now divide to approx. 5 glass bowls or champagne glasses. Immediately afterwards, mix the Quark-Flaxseed oil cream from Flaxseed oil, milk, honey and Quark. Finally, add 2 liqueur glasses of vodka or slibovitz or cherry brandy or rum into the Quark-Flaxseed oil cream. This Quark-Flaxseed oil mixture is evenly divided on the ready to-use bowls so that the Quark-Flaxseed oil cream partly sinks down in the middle. It is served after complete solidification.

Ice cream with cocoa

Ingredients:

- 3 tablespoons of Flaxseed oil, 3 tablespoons of milk,

- 1 tablespoon of honey, 100g of Quark, 100 g of hazelnuts,

- 2 tablespoons of cocoa

Preparation:

Quark, Flaxseed oil, milk and honey are mixed in the blender, then the hazelnuts are added, well blended and finally, cocoa is added to the mixture. Now pour the entire mixture into the ice-maker and place it in the fridge compartment of the refrigerator. This mixture with a nougat flavour gives the various combinations mentioned here the dark colour contrasts. For very ill people these preparations are very important, especially when there is a general lack of appetite.

(Oil-Protein Diet by Lothar Hirneise available at http://www.hirneise.com/page-8/page-19/)

ELDI oils

Dr. Budwig created unique ELDI oils, called electron differential oils after performing precise spectroscopic measurements of the light absorption in different oils - specifying that the oils contained pi-electron clouds from Flax oil, wheat germ oil plus vitamin-E in its natural complex, etheric oils and sulfhydryl groups.

Dr. Johanna Budwig said, "The sun is my preferred treatment modality, as is ELDI oil, used externally to stimulate the absorption of the long-wave band of the sun. I have used ELDI oils extensively since 1968 for body massage as well as in the selective application of oil packs. US pain institute has written somewhere: "What this crazy woman does with her ELDI oils, none of us manages to do via pain killers." Dr. Budwig has mentioned that if ELDI oil is not available, you may use Flax oil instead. You can buy ELDI oils at: www.sensei.de

Massage Benefits

Since ancient time massage has been part of cancer healing. Think of your lymphatics as a trash-disposal system for your body. Massage initiates lymphatic drainage, you push the trash out of your body and you're helping your immune system.

• Massage therapy is sometimes the first really pleasant touch a patient is able to experience.

• Massage also releases endorphins (our body's natural painkillers), stimulates lymph movement, and stretches tissues throughout the body. It's energizing, stimulating, and pretty good feeling.

ELDI oil plans:

A: For cancer patients in support of the energy level

    1. Full-body rubbings in the morning

    2. ELDI oil R enema with 200ml every 2-3 days

    3. Wrap at the "place of the happening"

B: For energetically weak patients

    1. Full-body rubbings in the morning and in the evening

    2. Enema: standard plan for ELDI oil R

    3. Wrap at the "place of the happening"

    4. Daily liver wrap with ELDI oil sage

Additional information:

Make sure that you make once a week an (deep/high) enema with water or coffee.

If you make daily coffee enemas, then start in the morning with the coffee enema and then with the ELDI R enema, but only if your energetic level allows you to make two enemas daily. Otherwise, only make the ELDI R enema. (Oil Protein Diet by Lothar Hirneise)

ELDI oils from SENSEI (www.sensei.de) are produced in a permanent cold chain in a European oil mill and marketed under the name of Electron Differentiation Oils. There are two qualities. A 6-star organic quality and a 5-star quality, which are produced exclusively for the IOPDF (www.iopdf.com).

Cost factor ELDI oils

Again and again we hear that for reasons of cost, patients use Flax seed oil instead of ELDI oil R for an enema. Please do not do so, because Flax seed oil does not react in the same way as ELDI oil R. Instead, use cheap ELDI oils from IOPDF or reduce the amount of oil.

Procedure –

Two times a day, i.e. morning and evening, rub ELDI Oil or Flax oil into the skin over the whole body, a bit more intensely on the shoulders, armpits and groin area (where plenty of lymphatic vessels are present) as well as the problem areas, such as the breast, stomach, liver, etc. Leave the oil on the skin for about 20 minutes and follow with a warm water shower without washing with soap. After 10 minutes take another shower, this time using a mild soap, and then relax for 15-20 minutes.

Once the body has been oiled and the ELDI Oil or Flax oil has penetrated the skin, the warm water will open the skin pores and the oil penetrates the skin more deeply. The second shower, where one washes with soap, cleanses the skin so that clothes and linen will not become overly soiled.

Oil Packs

Take a piece of cloth made of pure cotton. Cut to a size to fit the body part, such as the knee. Soak the cotton cloth with oil, place on the knee etc., cover it with a piece of polythene and wrap it up with an elastic bandage. Leave overnight. Remove in the morning and wash the knee; repeat in the evening. Keep applying the same procedure for weeks, you get good results. You also use Flax oil or castor oil for these local applications if you do not get ELDI oils . Dr Budwig generally recommended ELDI sage and should be used in the following indications:

- Tumours

- Painful skin areas

- Metastases

- Hepatic impairment and liver support

- Kidney problems

- Bladder disorders

- Intestinal cramps

- Lung disorders

- Bone disorders of all kinds

ELDI Oil Enema

Enemas are used in the Oil-Protein Diet exclusively for the energy intake and not for the purification of the intestine. Dr Budwig used to give ELDI oil or Flax oil enema to her serious patients. Budwig used to get immediate and miraculous results with the most seriously ill patients. Flax seed Oil enema also give similar results.

I recommend you to make the first enemas only with 100ml and then increase over several days to 250ml. Some patients have enemas with 500ml oil and positively reported on it. 500ml are however the absolute exception and mostly not necessary. Usually 250ml suffice.

Incidentally, smaller amounts are also easily introduced with an enema syringe instead of with an enema bucket. Enema syringes are available in sizes up to 350ml and are easy to handle.

Standard plan for ELDI oil R: Day 1 = 100ml, day 2 = 100ml, day 3 = 150ml, day 4 = 150ml, day 5 = 200ml, day 6 = 200ml and day 7 = 250ml.

From the seventh day, one remains at 250ml, and so long until the patient is significantly better. Then you can go back to 100ml - 150ml, always together with 1-2 daily whole body rubbings. (Oil Protein Diet by Lothar Hirneise)

Ingredients

- Enema pot

- Watch

- A bowl to collect oil when you are getting rid of bubbles.

- Towel and tissue

- RO filtered water

- ELDI oil or Flax oil

- Towel or Drip Stand

Procedure

Prepare a place near the toilet, so that if you can't hold the enema, you will be making a quick dash and the shorter distance is better.

Cleansing Enema with Plain water

First of all you should take a plain water enema. Purpose of this enema is cleaning of intestines. It is not a retention enema and is evacuated immediately. For this you may use 500-1000ml (2-4 cups) RO filtered water. As soon as the whole water is inside the rectum, go and sit on the commode and release the water slowly.

Take the oil enema immediately after the water enema

- Use advised (above) amount of ELDI or Flax oil. The oil should be at body temperature. The best test is to dip your little finger into the oil.

- Fill the oil into the enema pot. It takes at least 5 minutes for the bubbles to get out of the tube.

- The enema pot should be hanged on a drip stand about 2-3 feet above your body.

- You need to lubricate the nozzle and anus with Flax oil. When all is ready, lie on your right side in the fetal position. Insert the nozzle into the rectum slowly and carefully with your left hand, and un-pinch the tube.

- If you feel little uncomfortable when the oil is going in, pinch the tube, wait till the feeling passes away, then continue again.

- The oil is much more viscous and moves more slowly. You might need to hold the pot a bit higher to get it to run a bit quicker.

- Once the oil is in, wait and hold it for about 12 minutes. After that slowly turn yourself to left side and hold oil for another 12 minutes. You may listen to music while taking enema.

- When done, it is best to sit on the commode for about 15 minutes with something to read (Skelton).

Coffee Enema

Dr. Max Gerson introduced coffee enema back in the 1930s. In this enema about 500ml of coffee is pushed into rectum, this amount only reaches up to sigmoid colon. There is no loss of minerals and electrolytes in Coffee Enema because their absorption occurs well before sigmoid colon. Coffee enema is even safe for those who are 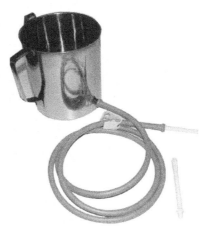 allergic to coffee because it is not absorbed into the systemic circulation. You may take this enema once or twice. It has the following benefits:

- Powerful and Natural Pain Reliever

- Cleansing - Coffee also acts as an astringent in the large intestine, helps cleanse the colon walls.

- Toxin Elimination - The major benefit of the coffee enema is elimination of toxins through the liver. Caffeine, theophylline and theobromine dilate the blood vessels and bile ducts, stimulate the liver to discharge more bile and boost the detoxifying process into high gear and heal inflammation. Indeed, endoscopic studies confirm they increase bile output.

- Stimulates Liver - Kahweol and cafestol palmitate found in coffee promote the activity of a key enzyme system called glutathione S-Transferase. This is an important mechanism in the detoxification of carcinogens, as the enzyme group is responsible for neutralizing free radicals. Coffee enema stimulates the activity of this system by 600- 700%.

Coffee Enema Procedure

- This enema is retained for 12-14 minutes, during this time blood circulates in liver three times and blood is purified. Coffee enema can be given several times a day, few patients take up to seven times a day. Normally if pain is not relieved it may be taken more than one time. You should relax while taking enema; you may listen to music or read newspaper while relaxing. The best time for coffee enema is either early morning after you passed motion or during the day time.

- Grind organic coffee beans. Put approx. 750ml of filtered water in a steal pan and bring it to boil. Add 2-5 heaped Tbsp coffee powder, 3 Tbsp is ideal. It is roughly 20-25grams. Let it continue to simmer for ten minutes or more and then turn off the burner. Allow it to cool down to a very comfortable, tepid temperature. Test it with your finger. It should be the same temperature as your body's temperature. Filter the coffee with fine mesh steal sieve into a jug. This is approximately 500ml.

- Pour 2 cups (500ml) of coffee into the enema pot. Be sure the plastic hose is clamped tightly. Now open the clamp and grasp, but do not close the clamp on the hose. Place the enema tip in the sink. Hold up the enema bag above the tip until the coffee begins to flow out. As soon as it starts flowing, quickly close the clamp. This expels any air in the tube.

- Lubricate the enema tip with a small amount of coconut oil or KY jelly. Create a comfortable and relaxing atmosphere. After a few days you will thoroughly enjoy this ritual.

- Light a candle, play some light music and most importantly, make sure you are comfortable and warm. We recommend placing a pillow with a washable cover under your head and lying down on an old towel.

- The position preferred is lying on your back. With the clamp closed hang the pot about 3 feet above your belly. We like to hang the enema pot on a drip stand.

- Insert the tip gently into anus and open the clamp slowly. You should relax and breathe. The coffee may take a few seconds to begin flowing. If you develop a cramp, close the hose clamp, turn from side to side and take a few deep breaths. The cramp will usually pass quickly. Usually nothing happens.

- When all the liquid is inside, close the clamp and remove it slowly. Retain the enema for 12- 14 minutes. You may remain lying on the floor.

- After 14 minutes or so, go to the toilet and empty your gut. Take your time. Wash the enema pot and tube thoroughly with soap and water.

- Take more potassium in the form of fruits and vegetable juices if you take coffee enema regularly (S.A.Wilsons.com).

Epsom bath

Detoxification of your body through bathing is an ancient remedy that anyone can perform in the comfort of your own home. Your skin is known as the third kidney, and toxins  are excreted through sweating. An Epsom salt bath is thought to assist your body in eliminating toxins as well as absorbing the magnesium and nutrients that are in the water. Soaking in Epsom salt actually helps replenish the body's magnesium levels, combating hypertension. The sulphate flushes toxins and helps form proteins in brain tissue and joints. Most of all, it will leave you relaxed, refreshed and awakened. Take it once a week or as advised.

Prepare your bath

- It is a 40 minutes ritual. The first 20 minutes are said to help your body remove the toxins, while the second 20 minutes are for absorbing the minerals from the water

- Fill your tub with comfortably hot water. Use a chlorine filter if possible.

- Add Epsom salt (Magnesium sulphate). For people 50 Kg and up, add 2 cups or more to a standard bath tub.

- Then add 2 cups or more of soda bicarb. It is known for its cleansing ability and even has anti-fungal properties. It also leaves skin very soft.

- Add 2-3 Tbsp ground ginger. While this step is optional, ginger can increase your heat levels, helping to sweat out more toxins. However, since it is heating the body, it may cause your skin to turn slightly red for a few minutes, so be careful with the amount you add. Depending on the capacity of your tub, anywhere from 1 Tbsp to 1/3 cup can be added (Hirneise).

- Add aromatherapy oils. Again optional, but there are many oils that will make the bath an even more pleasant and relaxing experience (such as lavender), as well as those that will assist in the detoxification process (tea tree or eucalyptus oil). Around 20 drops is sufficient for a standard bath.

- Swish all of the ingredients around in the tub, and then slip into the tub. You should start sweating within the first few minutes. If you feel too hot, start adding cold water into the tub until you cool off.

- Get out of the tub slowly and carefully. Your body has been working hard and you may get lightheaded or feel weak and drained. On top of that, the salts make your tub slippery, so stand with care.

- Drink plenty of water and relax in bed for a few minutes

Soda bicarb bath

Lothar Hirneise has given lot of importance to Soda bicarb bath. It is thought to assist you in eliminating toxins as well as making your body alkaline so your tumour cells may suffocate. Patient may take it once or even twice a day. Just add 2 cups of soda bicarb in your bath tub filled with warm water and relax in it for 30-40 minutes (Hirneise, 2005).

Sun Therapy

Getting an adequate amount of sunshine is a critical part of Budwig protocol. Once the body has acquired the right oil-protein balance with the Cottage Cheese and Flax oil, the body develops better capacity to absorb the healing photons from the sun. Remember that for healing of cancer high energy photons from the sun are very important. The sunshine is important to maintain adequate vitamin-D levels in our body. Vitamin-D is a powerful antioxidant that has been linked to preventing many diseases including cancer.

Dr. Budwig's focus was on the importance of photons from the sunbeams and their interaction with vital essential fats (linoleic and linolenic acid) in our body. It is the interaction of photons from the sun and the electrons in proper food that provide the synergistic effect on healing our body. Eating the electron rich Flax oil/Cottage Cheese mixture, must be connected with adequate exposure to sunlight.

There is nothing else on earth with a higher concentration of photons of the sun's energy than man. This concentration of the sun's energy is very much energetic point for humans, with their wave eminently suitable lengths - is improved when we eat electron rich essential oils, which in turn absorbs the photons in the form of electro-magnetic waves of sunbeams.

When you eat the FO/CC mixture, your body becomes a better antenna for the photons from the sunbeam. Your body develops a better ability to absorb the energy from the sun and Transfer it to your cells to perform their vital functions. You become energized at a deep level, and when this happens cancer is healed itself.

It is red light that penetrates deeper in the tissues. In 1968 Dr. Budwig used 695 nm ruby (red) lasers light with success to radiate healthy surrounding cancer tissues in cancer patients.

How long should you take this protocol?

If all is well patient feels better and tumour start to shrink within a 3 or 4 months, if he follows treatment religiously and honestly. He may be cured in one or two years. It is recommended that the Budwig protocol and full diet is followed for at least five years. Even after that he should maintain healthy eating and life style.

Dr. Budwig has clearly mentioned that if you do not get the desired success, do not blame the protocol, rather try to find out your mistakes and correct them. The threshold between winning and losing is very small, and even a minor mistake can unbalance the complete healing process.

Linomel

Linomel is an invention by Dr Budwig. Freshly crushed Flax seed is mixed with honey and milk powder so that the crushed Flax seed is more stable. There is no doubt that freshly crushed Flax seed is more valuable, but also has the disadvantage that you do it yourself and clean the grinder afterwards. That is why Linomel still has an existence right. Do not buy crushed Flax seed in the shop as the chance that these contain Tran's fatty acids is 100%.

Is there an alternative to Linomel?

Freshly crushed Flax seed is an alternative. This must be eaten immediately after the meal, otherwise it will oxidize.

Make your own Linomel. Mix 6 tablespoons freshly crushed Flax seed with a tablespoon of honey. Small tip: Grind the Flax seed, e.g. in a coffee grinder, and set the grinder to coarse. So it mixes better with the honey.

(Oil Protein Diet by Lothar Hirneise)

Daylight

Dr Budwig focused upon the importance of daylight to our health. It is not enough to absorb electrons only through food, but it is important that we feed ourselves so that our cells are able to absorb and process the light coming from the sun. The more sickly someone is, the sooner he is "in the house", which can be a catastrophic mistake. Especially when people are already in a very late stage of the illness, they are often not able to eat enough and good advice is then very difficult. In such cases, Dr Budwig advises to concentrate on the following three points:

- ELDI oils as whole body rubbings and if possible as enemas

- Only freshly squeezed juices and distributed as food throughout the day if possible the breakfast muesli in different variants

- Stay outside as much as possible

You will experience me to explain what to do next. I have been able to see in my life how Dr Budwig's theoretical considerations work when put to practice, if indeed, if they are consistently carried out. If you could experience such a case yourself, and how quickly it can be better for a seriously ill person, you can see Dr Budwig's words in a very different light.

But other great researchers had also dealt with the subject of light long before Dr Budwig. For example, the anthroposophist Rudolf Steiner wrote, about 50 years earlier that there is a fundamental being of our material existence of the earth, of which all materiality has come only through condensation. Every matter on earth is condensed light! There is nothing in material existence, which is something else than condensed light in some form. Wherever you go and feel matter, you have condensed light everywhere. Compressed light. Matter is light by its very nature. In as much as a man is a material being, he is woven of light. Rudolf Steiner and Dr Budwig have pointed out in their writings over and over again the importance of light and that we humans are now heliotropes, which need light and use light. But I have nowhere else than with Dr Budwig so clearly and understandably read, WHY this is and above all, how the charging of the life battery works and / or what importance mainly the linolenic acid or electron clouds play. Because it is so important, I would like to repeat here again: The sicklier someone is, the more he should be in the open." (Oil-Protein Diet by Lothar Hirneise)

Lani Maque heals his Pancreatic cancer

I have pancreatic cancer- stage 4 (mets to liver, L3 Lumbar, lungs and lymph node) diagnosed May 2018, Given 3 months to live. With God's help I'm still thriving. Budwig Protocol is one of my major protocol and helps me in my survival. At the moment, I'm stable and living a normal life I'm working and based in Singapore. God bless, miracles happen every day.

Lani Maque

Join
Our great Budwig Protocol Group on Facebook

I have a Budwig Protocol group on Facebook, which is the largest group on Budwig. There are more than 6500 members worldwide. You must join to this group. Miracles happen here every day. Lothar Herniese, 3E Center Germany, Dr. Jenkins, Budwig Center, Spain, Madam Sandra Olsen of Yahoo's flaxseedoil2, Arsula from US are members of my group.

The link is https://www.facebook.com/groups/budwig/

Disclaimer

This book is not intended to replace the advice and/or care of a qualified health care professional. Please do not try to self diagnose or self treat any disease. Seek professional help and consult your physician before making any dietary changes.

This book is not intended to provide medical advice and is sold with the understanding that the publisher and the author have neither liability nor responsibility to any person or entity with respect to loss, damage or injury caused or alleged to be caused directly or indirectly by the information contained in this book or the use of any products mentioned. Readers should not use any of the product discussed in this book without the advice of a medical profession.

The Food and Drug Administration has not approved the use of any of the natural treatments discussed in this book. This book, and the information contained herein, has not been approved by the Food and the Drug Administration.

Om Verma

My Books

Cancer - Cause and Cure

Based on Quantum Physics developed by Dr. Johanna Budwig

http://www.amazon.com/Cancer-Quantum-Physics-developed-Johanna-ebook/dp/B00P3Y7BYG

Book Description

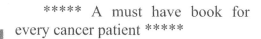

***** A must have book for every cancer patient *****

This book provides an introduction of Dr. Budwig's cancer research and treatment. Johanna Budwig (1908-2003) was nominated for the Nobel Prize seven times. She was one of Germany's leading scientists of the 20th Century, a biochemist and cancer specialist with a special interest in essential fats.

Otto Warburg proved that prime cause of cancer oxygen-deficiency in the cells. In absence of oxygen cells ferment glucose to produce energy, lactic acid is formed as a by-product of fermentation. He postulated that sulfur containing protein and some unknown fat is required to attract oxygen in the cell.

In 1951 Dr. Budwig developed Paper Chromatography to identify fats. With this technique she proved that electron rich highly unsaturated Linoleic and Linolenic fatty acids were the undiscovered mysterious decisive fats in respiratory enzyme function that Otto Warburg had been unable to find. She studied

127

the electromagnetic function of pi-electrons of the linolenic acid in the membranes of the microstructure of protoplasm, for all nerve function, secretions, mitosis, as well as cell break-down. This immediately caused lot of excitement in the scientific community. New doors could open in Cancer research. Hydrogenated fats, including all Tran's fatty acids were proved as respiratory poisons.

Then Budwig decided to have human trials and gave flaxseed oil and quark to cancer patients. After three months, the patients began to improve in health and strength, the yellow green substance in their blood began to disappear, tumours gradually receded and at the same time the nutrients began to rise. This way Dr. Budwig had found a cure for cancer. It was a great victory and first milestone in the battle against cancer. Her treatment protocol is based on the consumption of flax seed oil with low fat cottage cheese, raw organic diet, mild exercise, and the healing powers of the sun. She treated approx. 2500 cancer patients during a 50 year period with this protocol till her death with over 90% documented success.

She was nominated 7 times for Nobel Prize but with a condition that she will use chemotherapy and radiotherapy with her protocol. They did not want to collapse the 200 billion dollar business over night. She always refused to support the damaging chemo and radio for the sake of humanity.

The book also, describes about rare and miraculous herbs used in the treatment of Cancer like Turmeric, Black seed, Ginger, Mistle Toe, Aloe vera, Echinacea, Lobelia, Essiac Tea, Pau d'arco Tea, Dandelion, Milk Thistle.

~~**~~

Cancer Cure Is Found: Laetrile is the answer

https://www.amazon.com/Cancer-Cure-Found-Laetrile-answer/dp/1797710206/

CANCER CURE IS FOUND

During 1950, a biochemist Dr. Ernest T. Krebs Jr., isolated a new vitamin from bitter apricot kernel that he called 'B-17' or 'Laetrile'. He conducted further lab animal and culture experiments to conclude that laetrile would be effective in the treatment of cancer. He proposed that cancer was caused by a deficiency of Vitamin B 17 (Laetrile, Amygdaline). Laetrile is a concentrated and purified form of vitamin B17. After a lot of research, he had finally developed a specific protocol

Dr. Om Verma

Cancer Cure Is Found

Laetrile is the answer

to treat cancer. Laetrile Therapy combines Laetrile with nutritional supplements and a healthy diet to create a potent treatment that fights cancer cells while helping to strengthen the body's immune system.

Vitamin B-17, which is present in several different foods, consists of a locked substance which comprises two units' glucose, one unit Benzaldehyde and one unit cyanide. When B17 comes in contact with a cancer cell it is unlocked by a hormone found only in the cancer cell, and becomes a lethal chemical bomb which destroys the cancer cell. Healthy cells do not cause breakdown of B17. Cancer is unknown to people living in areas with food products rich in B-17, and the population lives to a remarkably high age. Apparently nature has provided us with an ingenious defence against cancer, and it is an ordinary nutrient in our food. These are, amongst others nuts, seeds, vegetables, and in particular apricot kernels.

At present, patients listen or read a lot about Laetrile treatment, but usually they don't get precise and to the point information about what are the exact components of this protocol, where to get Laetrile injections and supplements, what to take, what not to take, what are the doses, how long to take the treatment, what diet they have to follow, etc. In this book, I have explained the protocol in detail proposed by Dr. Krebs. I have given every minute detail about Laetrile, other nutritional supplements and diet in this book. After reading this book patients can buy Laetrile injections, tablets and other nutritional supplements from the reliable sources (given in the book) and conduct the treatment under the supervision of their family doctor. Dr. Philip E. Binzel was personally trained by Dr. Ernest T. Kreb Jr. about everything of this treatment. Dr. Binzel had been using Laetrile therapy in the treatment of cancer patients since the mid 1970s. His record of success was astounding. Testimonies of his patients are also included in this book.

~~**~~

Awesome Flax: A Book by Flax Guru
Flax seed- Miraculous Anti-ageing Divine Food
https://www.amazon.com/Awesome-Flax-Book-Guru-ebook/dp/B00PUUIR0K

What is Flax seed and how can it benefit me? I was faced with this question when I started hearing about Flax seed not long ago. It became a 'buzz word' in society and seems to be making great role in increased health for many. I wanted to join that wagon of wellness and so I researched until I felt satisfied that it could help me, too. Here are my findings.

Flax seeds are the hard, tiny seeds of Linum usitatissimum, the Flax plant, which has been widely used for thousands of years as a source of food and clothing. Flax seeds have become very popular recently, because they are a richest source of the Omega 3 essential fatty acid; also known as Alpha Linolenic Acid (ALA) and lignans. People in the new millennium may see Flax seed as an important new FOOD SUPER STAR. In fact, there's nobody who won't benefit by adding Flax seed to his or her diet. Even Gandhi wrote: "Wherever Flax seed becomes a regular food item among the people, there will be better health."

Flax seed contains 30-40% oil (including 36-50% alpha linolenic acid, 23-24% linoleic acid- Omega-6 fatty acids and oleic acids), mucilage (6%), protein (25%), Vitamin B group, lecithin, selenium, calcium, folate, magnesium, zinc, iron, carotene, sulfur, potassium, phosphorous, manganese, silicon, copper, nickel, molybdenum, chromium, and cobalt, vitamins A and E and all essential amino acids.

Other fatty acids, omega-6's, is abundant in vegetable oils such as corn, soybean, safflower, and sunflower oils as well as in the many processed foods made from these oils. Omega-6 fatty acids have stimulating, irritating and inflammatory effect while omega-3 fatty acids have calming and soothing effect on our body. Our bodies function best when our diets contain a well-balanced ratio of these fatty acids, meaning 1:1 to 4:1 of omega-6 and omega-3. But we typically eat 10 to 30 times more omega-6's than omega-3's, which is a prescription for trouble. This imbalance puts us at greater risk for a number of serious illnesses, including heart disease, cancer, stroke, and arthritis. As the most abundant plant source of omega-3 fatty acids, Flax seed helps restore balance and lets omega-3's do what they're best at: balancing the immune system, decreasing inflammation, and lowering some of the risk factors for heart disease.

One way that Omega 3 essential fatty acid known as Alpha Linolenic Acid ALA helps the heart is by decreasing the ability of platelets to clump together. Flax seed helps to lower high blood pressure, clears clogged coronaries, lowers high blood cholesterol, bad LDL cholesterol and triglyceride levels and raises good HDL cholesterol. It can relieve the symptoms of Diabetes Mellitus. It lowers blood sugar level. Flax seed help fight obesity. Adding Flax seed to foods creates a feeling of satiation. Furthermore, Flax seed stokes the metabolic processes in our cells. Much like a furnace, once stoked, the cells generate more heat and burn calories.

Flax seeds are the most abundant source of lignans. Lignans are plant-based compounds that can block estrogen activity in cells, reducing the risk of Breast, Uterus, Colon and Prostate cancers. According to the US Department of Agriculture, Flax seed contains 27 identifiable cancer preventative compounds. Lignans in Flax seeds are 200 to 800 times more than any other lignan source. Lignans are phytoestrogens, meaning that they are similar to but weaker than the estrogen that a woman's body produces naturally. Therefore, they may also help alleviate menopausal discomforts such as hot flashes and vaginal dryness. They are also antibacterial, antifungal, and antiviral.

Because they are high in dietary fibber, ground Flax seeds can help ease the passage of stools and thus relieve constipation, haemorrhoids and diverticular disease. Taken for inflammatory bowel disease, Flax seed can help to calm inflammation and repair any intestinal tract damage.

Secrets of Success: Smart way to success for every student

http://www.amazon.com/Secrets-Success-Smart-success-student-ebook/dp/B00Q3IIVAO/

Normally people think that memory, intelligence or learning ability is a God gift and it is not possible to further improve or increase the brain powers. We take it for granted that it will remain as it is gifted to us by God. But the truth is just opposite. Understand that as you go to gym for workout to develop your six pack abs, feed your body with muscle building food and get sharp sculpted body shape. Friends, believe me if muscle can be built and remodelled, then why not your brain's hardware and circuit boards. If you feed your brain with proper food it  needs, follow simple instructions and take advantage of neurobics or mnemonics, you can immensely increase your brain's abilities.

We have tremendous powers locked inside our brains, but we are not using them to full extent. Dr. William James, considered the father of modern psychology, pointed out that "the average human being uses only 10 percent of his mental capacity." We still have to find out how much power or secrets are hidden in our brain.

Nowadays scientists have discovered mysterious techniques and nutrients to boost our brain powers. Today I shall raise curtains from all these secrets; I shall disclose all hidden tricks and tips. Today you are going to learn how you're CPU, the brain tightly packed in a bony cabinet, functions. I teach you how each component and microprocessors works and how the best insulation material can be prepared. I also disclose the right technique to sharpen your brain and to make you an intelligent and successful scholar.

Today you will learn how to crack every examination you face, solve every question, defeat every opponent and get highest possible marks. You are going to write new equation of education and success.

Friends, new boundaries and horizon of success is ready to welcome you. Today we shall discuss in detail about some great nutrients and supplements to boost your memory, learning, imagination, creativity and concentration. If you follow our suggestions and apply simple tricks you achieve a successful personality. This short e-book is going to prove a turning point in your life. Wish you luck. Visit us at http://memboy.blogspot.in

~~**~~

Multiple Myeloma New Horizon
With Orthodox and Alternative Treatments
https://www.amazon.com/Multiple-Myeloma-New-Horizon-Alternative/dp/1797876015/

I have written this book so that the patients suffering from multiple myeloma can understand the disease in detail and choose a suitable treatment for them. This book provides detailed information about the clinical symptoms, complications, diagnosis, staging and treatments. In the last 15 years there has been considerable research and progress in the field of clinical studies, aetiology, pathology, diagnosis and treatment of multiple myeloma. Even if we do not have the cure of this disease, but still it is one of the highly treatable disease today. Today we have new and effective medicines, which work in a much better way. There are new treatments for bone lesions and fractures. There are new resources for the treatment of its complications. Not long ago, life of a Myeloma patient was miserable, confined to a wheelchair and he barely survived 2-3 years. At present time, Multiple Myeloma patients are surviving 10 years or more and are living comfortable life. The lifestyle of the patient is getting happier and convenient.

In this book, I have written in detail about Orthodox and Alternative Treatment (Budwig Protocol, which is the best alternative treatment and gives authentic success). Patient can carefully select the right treatment for him. This book has up to date information.

The End

Pancreatic Cancer

Contents

1

Healing with Crystals

Facing Everyday Life with the Power of Crystals and Stones

Learning about crystals while seeking to embody their wisdom will allow you to connect with their subtle energy and subsequent healing benefits. You will become open to new and evolved ways of perceiving, thinking, and absorbing new information, which further activates your higher mind or Higher Self, awakening you to the unity and beauty of the natural world. This is where you can be open to life's deeper meanings and mysteries. Interacting with crystals on a daily or cyclic basis amplifies your electromagnetic energy field, which, in turn, will spark a genuine desire and passion to learn about new topics and pathways to healing. Below, I've included *three of the best crystals* for some of life's most common challenges.

Facing Change

1. **Smoky Quartz**: A crystal of new beginnings, change, and potential, Smoky Quartz helps you accept and embrace your shadow so you can find your light self. It symbolizes transformation, new growth, and aligning with your highest potential. Smoky Quartz transmutes, alchemizes, and allows you to explore your wounds and traumas, without judgment. This allows you to release toxicity, heal your shadow self, and integrate missing parts into your holistic personality.

2. **Malachite**: Powerful for positive alchemy combined with light magic - creativity, manifestation, understanding sacred and universal laws, etc. - Malachite enhances transformation and change on deep levels. It's emotionally and psychologically grounding, stimulating, and balancing, as well as soothing and cleansing. It's an intensely healing stone for new beginnings, yet simultaneously gentle and serene.

3. **Green Aventurine**: Green Aventurine amplifies healing, harmony, and transformation. Potent vibrations for self-care and self-love, in addition to harmonious relationships - family, platonic, professional, and business - are part of Green Aventurine's healing properties. Thus, it's ideal for any life event or situation that requires personal growth. This gemstone for the Heart chakra inspires transcendence, i.e., letting go of toxic cycles and outgrown chapters.

Health and Wellbeing

1. Rose Quartz: For the heart, Rose Quartz increases vibrations of love, compassion, and empathy, which makes it ideal for living a happy and long life. Nurturing, empathy, tolerance, universal and selfless love, friendship, devotional energies, caring, forgiveness, and patience are all ideal for longevity. Holistic wellbeing is tied to a strong and healthy Heart chakra, which in turn, affects the physical heart. Rose Quartz balances, soothes, and nurtures, as well as promoting emotional calmness, psychological health, and spiritual and physical harmony. These all increase health and good fortune.

2. Amazonite: Amazonite is a subtle yet equally powerful healer, which also clears and aligns your chakras. It unblocks negative energy and repressed emotions in the chakras, as well as inspiring truth, honesty, self-love, eloquence, and integrity; all qualities for a happy life. Amazonite is a soothing stone that balances yin or feminine and masculine or yang energies. Thus, it's great for holistic healing, inner balance, and establishing and maintaining equilibrium. Further, it can help you see multiple points of view - excellent for a healthy mind and psychological functioning, which in turn, leads to an effective mind, body, and spirit connection. It dispels negative energy while protecting you from electromagnetic harm too.

3. Fluorite: Fluorite cleanses the aura, inspires higher truth, and activates consciousness, as well as shielding and protecting you from harm, psychic attack, and electromagnetic threat. This allows for a powerful mind, body, and soul connection. Neutralizing negative energy while strengthening psychic and intuitive gifts in such a way sparks longevity, life force, and inner harmony. Wholeness can be achieved. Fluorite is known for having a positive effect on the immune system, coupled with promoting a positive mindset. It is also believed to restructure faulty DNA!

Difficult Family/Friends Changes

1. Rhodonite: A stone of love, friendship, emotional warmth, and grace, Rhodonite is perfect for dealing with family and friendship challenges. It inspires elegance, confidence, and decision-making, increases calmness, tact, and diplomacy, and aligns you with your higher mind, your Higher Self. It promotes compassion, emotional intelligence, and depth, so you can see things clearly while responding instead of reacting to triggers or wounds. It's ideal for dealing with pain, sadness, and personal triggers in the right way, with caring, compromise, and kindness. As a stone of compassion and love, it's one of the best for all hardships, challenges, and imbalances in intimate relationships. It also sparks awareness of your inner path, purpose, and destiny, which helps you ascertain the right choices to make in your personal life. Further, it can help with emotional shock, abuse, and panic, as well as codependency, unforgiveness, and intolerance.

2. Moonstone: Moonstone is beautiful for emotional harmony, clarity, and balance. It amplifies selflessness, compassion, empathy, fortune, hope, and joy, in addition to self-knowledge, purity, and ancient wisdom. It sparks instincts and intuition for correct and kind decision-making, while stimulating spiritual sight, strength, and courage. Moonstone is perfect for mindful and empathic communication. Feelings of being loved, seen, and protected expand, and coupled with boundaries, this makes it ideal for difficult conversations with friends and family. Moonstone enhances intimacy, self-care, universal love, motherly instincts, and inner balance and harmony that reflects outwards.

3. Amethyst: Known as the Psychic's Stone or BS detector, Amethyst is highly effective for seeing through illusions. This means uncovering mistruths, seeing through deception, uncovering manipulation and hidden motives, becoming clear about boundaries, and ascertaining truth. These qualities are needed for honesty, transparency, and harmony in relationships. Also, Amethyst expands psychic gifts, combined with intuition at the highest levels. Amethyst sparks truth, self-knowledge, higher wisdom, fresh perspectives, and multidimensional awareness, as well as connecting you with a higher power for unity, connection, and authenticity. As the BS detector crystal, you can get to the root of anything that's been troubling your spirit, in addition to being more accountable as to your own follies and discrepancies.

Job/Business Challenges

1. Selenite: Selenite sparks the Crown chakra and cosmic consciousness, bringing some much-needed awareness into your business and job dealings. It activates subtle perception, intuition, and extrasensory abilities for truth and wisdom. Selenite promotes tranquility, calmness, and serenity for dealing with stresses and challenges with humility. Integrity, modesty, and diplomacy expand, as do peace of mind, clear sight, and faith that all will work out as it should. Selenite encourages honesty and nobility on the highest planes, bringing natural order and justice to external states of affairs. Other healing qualities include positive thinking, seeing the big picture, purification, mental clarity, non-judgement, and a peaceful and meditative outlook on life.

2. Citrine: Known as the Stone of Prosperity, Citrine enhances success, wealth, fortune, luck, inner strength, courage, and self-esteem, as well as manifestation abilities. It's the gemstone to turn to for help with business and professional challenges, because it clears pathways to success and abundance. Citrine can inspire confidence, self-empowerment, and freedom from fear in all your work dealings. It encourages optimism, happiness, protection, the positive pursuit of pleasure, generosity, kindness, and truth. It activates self-alignment, self-knowledge, and integrity, in addition to spiritual sight, warmth, and sociability. It energizes, cleanses, soothes, and harmonizes your personal energy for professional victory! Social anxiety, stress, and fears and phobias can be overcome.

3. Pyrite: Also known as Fool's Gold, Pyrite is similar to Citrine, but also brings the qualities of logic, higher intelligence, elevated learning and perception, channeling abilities, and protection from harm in a work setting. It's perfect for all challenges, hardships, and setbacks in professional activities, and at home if you work from a laptop or similar. Pyrite further increases psychic development, intellect, inspiration, modesty, integrity, and memory, as well as motivating you into action. It shields and projects you while stimulating mindfulness, communication, and self-evolution. Ancient Incans used Pyrite for divination and meditation.

Loss of A Loved One

1. Opal: Opal helps with pain and loss on a deep level because it stimulates love, peace, faith, consciousness, and loyalty. It encourages you to reflect, contemplate, and introspect with self-compassion and forgiveness. Opal assists in releasing emotional baggage, sincerity, feelings, depth and vulnerability, combined with inner strength, and freedom of thought and expression. It heals, soothes, and inspires growth and self-evolution on multiple planes. It intensifies emotions while cleansing and purging tricky ones. Problem-solving, imagination, self-worth, alignment with your true self, and creativity expand, qualities which are essential for the after-the-healing stages of loss. Opal brings faithfulness, optimism, creative visions, psychic gifts, and spontaneity for recovery after heartache, further amplifying independence, emotional calmness, and self-sovereignty.

2. Black Onyx: Black Onyx inspires strength, stamina, self-control, healing, and grounding, helping you find your center in times of hardship and struggle. It is ideal for loss and heartbreak or heartache, due to its immense strength-bringing nature. It grounds, stabilizes, and soothes your mood, as well as tricky emotions. It enhances happiness, good fortune, and wisdom for the next best course of action for you. Overall, this is a beautifully serene yet enduring stone for healing and new beginnings.

3. Angelite: Finally, Angelite increases strength, creativity, consciousness, peace, healing, and telepathy. It promotes psychic gifts, inspiration, clairvoyance, inner guidance, self-mastery, alignment with your true path, and faith. Angelite puts you in touch with celestial and heavenly guides, the realm of the archangels and angels, and your spirit team. It can connect you to an ethereal and spiritual world where hardships and struggles of the earthly reality seem void or mundane. Angelite achieves this without dismissing or denying your emotions, feelings, and sensitivities. Vulnerabilities and authentic emotions and thoughts can be explored without fear. It additionally facilitates spirit journeys and astral travel, while energizing forgiveness, deep healing, and soul cleansing. It transmutes pain and anger into joy and letting go... a powerful gift to possess when moving forward with your life. Inspiration, peace, tranquility, rebirth, transformation, and personal alchemy expand, further awakening the Throat chakra so you can express your emotions and communicate effectively, say, with a therapist or counselor.

Crystal Specifics: Deepening Your Healing Journey

There are six Lattice patterns you should be aware of if you wish to deepen your crystal journey:

Hexagonal: these have an interior structure that resembles a 3D hexagon, and they help with manifestation, consciousness, and Higher Self-awareness.

Isometric: these have an interior cubic structure, and they amplify positive energy flow, improve self-esteem and wellbeing, and increase personal power and charisma.

Monoclinic: these crystals have a 3D parallelogram structure, and they are protective, shielding, and stabilizing.

Orthorhombic: these are crystals with diamond-shaped crystalline patterns, and they cleanse, clear, and remove blockages.

Tetragonal: these have a rectangular interior structure, and they attract, increase abilities linked to the universal laws, and expand Third Eye abilities and power.

Triclinic: these have an interior structure with three inclined axes, and they protect you from unwanted energies and shield you in times of trauma or crisis, as well as enhancing the qualities you do want.

There are also different types of crystals. These are:

Crystal: A mineral that has a crystalline interior structure.

Gem: A cut and polished mineral, crystal, or rock stone.

Mineral: A naturally occurring substance with a specific chemical composition and highly ordered structure, which is not crystalline.

Rock: A combination of minerals.

Finally, crystals are used in technology, an area of exploration that can deepen your understanding of their healing properties!

- In World War II, the military used Quartz oscillators to control the frequencies of their two-way radio transmissions. The oscillators were highly efficient, effective, and precise, yet very difficult to mass-produce. This information was reported by an article in the IEEE Transactions on Ultrasonics, Ferroelectrics, and Frequency Control.
- According to the Minerals Education Coalition's Mineral Resources Database, manufacturers use electronics-grade manufactured Quartz in cell phones, computer circuits, and similar devices and equipment.
- Something a bit more well-known, I believe! Quartz is used in watches, due to the precision of its oscillators; Quartz is so interconnected, entwined, with the earth's electromagnetic energy field, that it is accurate to the second.

Crystal Water and Gem Essences

In ancient times, various cultures were aware of the power of crystals. Ancient Egyptians had dream temples where they would place large crystal geodes and structures for enhanced lucid dreaming, and intuitive capabilities. They knew that the crystals emitted unique vibrations that could increase innate healing powers, raise inner vibrations, and spark higher consciousness... Many cultures and countries have used crystals in such ways, or at least been knowledgeable about their healing properties and metaphysical powers. In more modern times, scientists chose to power watches with Quartz crystal, due to the unique gravitational effect it has with the Earth's energy field.

In this respect, we should turn our attention to one of our planet's "ultimate truths;" that water is the seed of life, water is the divine source of creation and consciousness. It's the element of sacred knowledge, ancient wisdom, spiritual powers, subconscious energy, and powerful instincts, intuition, and divine law. Water is all of these things, and it's in both our bodies and our sustaining planet! In high quantities.

So, drinking crystal-infused water is one thing you should definitely start doing if you wish to find lasting peace, internal happiness, and prosperity in life. The Egyptians, for instance, who had a very good quality of life, in addition to having access to advanced ancient knowledge regarding longevity, health, and spiritual enlightenment, had an advanced system of healing using gemstones. Ayurvedic medicine that originated in India also uses gemstones. Gems are ground into a very fine powder and mixed with liquid, which the patient then takes in prescribed dosages. Boiling gemstones in spring water also produces the same effects.

Drinking crystal water allows the crystal's aura to interact with ours, so a synchronization occurs, whereby we - the drinkers - receive the healing properties of the crystal. The subtle, spiritual, and energetic healing powers interact with our inner waters, activating cellular memory that occurs on the superconscious planes. Remember the subtle bodies, how each interacts; you have the physical body, then the etheric replica, then the astral, emotional, and mental bodies, which "converse" with the physical body below and higher bodies up above... Then, you have the spiritual body and finally the soul and causal planes. Consciousness connects them all. Consuming crystal-infused water or gem essences allows your cells and DNA to absorb the metaphysical healing powers of the crystal. Over time, you build up strength, power, and advanced conscious awareness. Drinking crystal water on a daily or cyclic (weekly, New and Full Moons, etc) basis sparks your soul body, while connecting you to your spiritual body. In this day and age, the spiritual body seems to be the missing link! In other words, we tend to be either more physical - sporty or sexual - or emotional - empathic or sensitive - or psychological - mental or analytical. It's rare to find a balanced and integrated being, i.e., someone whole, someone who has achieved inner harmony and equilibrium. Well, this has been the case up until now.

Crystal Water: Your Route to Super-consciousness

Crystal water is vital for holistic wellbeing and leading a beautiful, abundant, and blissful life. It affects all the planes and bodies, providing healing and balance to your aura, soul, emotional self, psychological self, spirit body, and physical vessel. It's a gem! Excuse the pun.

How to make crystal water:

Making crystal water is very easy. First, make sure your crystal is cleansed in water, charged in sunlight (or moonlight if the gem holds a particularly feminine energy), and either programmed, smudged, or grounded in earth. Remember that the first two methods, cleansing and charging, are primary and essential; the others are secondary or additional.

Place your purified and activated crystal in a bottle, container, or large bowl of mineral, spring, mountain, purified, or reverse osmosis water. These are the best types. The container should be non-metallic. If you can only source tap water, check that it is safe to consume. Leave your crystal in the water for anywhere between 12 and 24 hours. You can also keep your crystal in the water until all the water, essential life force, is consumed. That's it! Very easy and simple, yet highly effective and powerful.

Crystal water can be consumed within one week of its creation. It's not advised to leave it any longer than seven days.

*Crystals that should **not** be infused in water:*

In the crystal world, there are some crystals that are considered dangerous to put in water, even to cleanse for purification purposes. This is due to something known as the MOHS scale. The Mohs scale measures crystals' hardiness - how durable and strong the crystal is. Generally, crystals with a 5→ (below 5) ranking should *not* be put in water. These include: Kyanite, Fluorite, Azurite, Malachite, Shungite, Coral, Pearl, Jet, Chrysocolla, and Amber.

You can consult this professional guide for further information and clarity:

https://www.gemsociety.org/article/select-gems-ordered-mohs-hardness

Benefits of crystal water:

- Strengthens the immune system to build up the body's defenses against colds and flu.
- Removes toxins and impurities from the bloodstream.
- Neutralizes mental distortions and alleviates distorted and faulty beliefs and blockages.
- If charged in sunlight, it has a solarizing effect.
- If charged in moonlight, it has a lunarizing effect.

- Inner frequencies that have become muddied with toxic mindsets or behaviors can be released.
- It provides energy, vitality, and clear sight.
- It sparks intuition and psychic abilities.
- It activates consciousness through its link to the subtle energy bodies.
- Helps to protect you from negative energy, psychic attack, and electromagnetic harm.
- It can aid in amplifying other essences and tonics, such as flower essences, vitamins, and herbal elixirs.
- It can awaken dormant gifts, hidden memories, and ancient wisdom linked to the multidimensional planes.
- Over time, it can restructure DNA in profoundly positive ways, such as by awakening knowledge and talents linked to your soul's purpose or life plans!

Gem Essences: A Longevity Alternative

Gem essences are very similar to crystal water, except that they can be kept for much longer, weeks to months longer, in fact. Gem essences are a 50:50 water-alcohol solution. The process for making them is the same as for crystal water, only once the crystal has charged the water, you *remove* the crystal. Then, you mix the crystallized water solution with alcohol, preferably pure vodka. Whisky or rum can also work, but vodka is the best option. The solution should be 50:50. Gem essences can be kept in tincture bottles or larger bottles and used over longer periods of time; you add a few drops to a cold drink like water, organic juice, or cold herbal tea, and then drink it. Gem essences should be kept in a fridge or a cold and dry place.

What's so special about gem essences? They restructure your DNA! Providing you with a daily or cyclic dose of vibration-raising goodness... Over time, this changes your energetic blueprint, increasing zest, intuition, creative life force, passion, health, positivity, inner peace, inspiration, and any quality associated with the gemstone.

Gem essences are fun because, similar to flower essences or herbal remedies, you can start to develop a personal connection with your crystals. For example, taking Rose Quartz essence on a Friday, Venus' day, or over a particular romantic New Moon period... Or consuming Garnet essence when you need some fire, spark, and passion in your life, such as going on a hot date! Or for a business meeting.

Here are some unique ideas for using gem essences.

SUNDAY: A day for self-alignment and healing

Sunday is associated with the Sun, dominance, masculinity, strength, willpower, self-esteem, ambition, and creativity, as well as potent life force, prosperity, success, energy, positivity, vitality, renewal, and good luck. Taking gem essences on Sunday can increase and awaken all of these qualities!

: Amber, Sapphire, Clear Quartz, Tiger's Eye, Sunstone, Peridot, Topaz, Carnelian, Red Jasper, Citrine, Rose Quartz, and Green Aventurine

Sunday Affirmations:

- 'I am courageous, confident, and expressive in everything I do.'
- 'I align with my soul path and plan, becoming a way-shower for others through my courage.'
- 'I act with dignity, nobility, and boldness, shining a light on everything wishing to come to conscious light.'
- 'I am confident, passionate, ambitious, self-assured, and direct. I live with high self-esteem and humility.'
- 'I embrace my power and authority to inspire, teach, and lead.'

MONDAY: A day for self-reflection and inspiration

Monday is associated with the Moon, imagination, inspiration, empathy, emotional intelligence, nurturing, caring, compassion, sensitivity, and sacred knowledge, as well as instincts, feelings, divine law and order, spiritual powers, psychic gifts, receptivity, personal magnetism, and the subconscious mind.

Crystals for Monday: Moonstone, Pearl, Smoky Quartz, Amethyst, Aquamarine, Carnelian, Sugilite, Celestite, Selenite, Fluorite, and Tiger's Eye

Monday Affirmations:

- 'I aim to be more gentle, gracious, and sensitive so I can live abundantly.'
- 'I choose emotional intelligence, sensitivity, and empathy in every moment.'
- 'Selflessness, grace, and compassion are doorways to my highest potential.'

- 'I reflect unconditional love combined with feminine instincts.'
- 'I am nurturing, caring, wise, patient, and empathic. I choose harmony over conflict and chaos.'

TUESDAY: A day for passion and action

Tuesday is associated with Mars, passion, vitality, ambition, competition, action, a warrior mindset, and masculine sexuality, as well as will, strength, excitement, commitment to a cause, courage, boldness, confidence, assertiveness, and enthusiasm.

Crystals for Tuesday: Obsidian, Bloodstone, Garnett, Jet, Sapphire, Hematite, Moldavite, Sardonyx, Carnelian, and Ruby

Tuesday Affirmations:

- 'I embrace my wild side so I can shine in my career and professional life.'
- 'Sex, intimacy, and playfulness are gateways to a more balanced, holistic, and happy life.'
- 'Energy, life force, and enthusiasm serve my ambitions and passions well.'
- 'Becoming conscious of my triggers allows me to live calmly and with peaceful intent, instead of choosing reactions and explosions.'
- 'My will, motivation, and intentions are important. I am the boss of my own life.'

WEDNESDAY: A day for communication and self-expression

Wednesday is associated with Mercury, communication, intellect, wit, logic, self-expression, intelligence, and cerebral gifts, as well as technology, transportation, memory, curiosity, inquisitiveness, sociability, personal power, psychological ambition, and messages from the spirit.

<u>Crystals for Wednesday</u>: Blue Lace Agate, Sodalite, Sapphire, Amazonite, Amber, Lapis Lazuli, Blue Kyanite, Chalcedony, and Aquamarine

<u>Wednesday Affirmations</u>:

- 'I work on my communication skills so I can master my relationships, both personal and professional.'
- 'Self-expression, art, and imagination are keys to prosperity and wellbeing.'
- 'Mindful and empathic communication is ideal for prosperity and harmonious connections.'
- 'I choose to balance healthy solitude, rest, and introspection with sociability.'
- 'I embrace the inner curious adventurer and traveler in me, opening myself up to new cultural and educational paths.'

THURSDAY: A day for luck and expansion

Thursday is associated with Jupiter, luck, expansion, abundance, philosophy, higher learning, spiritual ideals, philosophy, and big-picture thinking, as well as adventure, travel, cultural pursuits, boldness, courage, sovereignty, fortune, fame, independence, and higher truth.

<u>Crystals for Thursday</u>: Topaz, Aventurine, Carnelian, Peacock Ore, Tiger's Eye, Turquoise, Amber, Citrine, Amethyst, Sugilite, and Yellow Sapphire

<u>Thursday Affirmations</u>:

- 'I am a lucky and prosperous soul when I choose optimism and positivity.'

- 'I embrace my need for travel, change, and adventure, as this keeps my spirit alive.'
- 'I align with an ambitious path for healing, friendships, and financial expansion.'
- 'Creative and artistic projects keep me both grounded and energized. I keep my energy levels high for success.'
- 'Philosophy, spirituality, idealism, independence, and courage to shine and expand are the qualities I choose to embody.'

FRIDAY: A day for pleasure and romance

Friday is associated with Venus, romance, warmth, sensitivity, female sexuality, beauty, fertility, pleasure, and sensuality, as well as wealth, intimacy, attraction, love, self-care, the arts, eroticism, devotion, passion, desire, allure, fun, and friendship.

Crystals for Friday: Emerald, Jade, Tree Moss Agate, Ruby, Rhodonite, Rose Quartz, Citrine, Moonstone, Pearl, Celestite, Carnelian, and Green Aventurine

Friday Affirmations:

- 'I choose love and intimacy for holistic health and wellbeing.'
- 'I accept I have a romantic and wild side that needs both liberation and expression.'
- 'Pleasure is a direct gateway to divinity, as long as it's mindful and rooted in loving affection.'
- 'Self-care serves me mentally, emotionally, physically, and spiritually. I honor my body's needs and desires.'
- 'Exploring the wounds of my past allows me to move past sadness, grief, and heartbreak.'

SATURDAY: A day for self-authority and accomplishment

Saturday is associated with Saturn, authority, discipline, structure, rules, regulations, oppressive regimes, positive enforcements, time, and karma, as well as society, laws, order, power positions, achievement, accomplishments, societal success, responsibilities, prestige, and practicalities.

Crystals for Saturday: Black Tourmaline, Red Jasper, Hematite, Jet, Garnett, Smoky Quartz, Onyx, Obsidian, Blue Sapphire, Lolite, Amethyst, and Shungite

Saturday Affirmations:

- 'I step into self-leadership for ultimate living; personal power and authority are my mantras.'
- 'I choose to be direct and gentle, courageous and humble, and electric and magnetic in equal measure.'
- 'My life is aligned to a higher path, a long-term plan of action where vision, hard work, and success are the foundations.'
- 'I choose smaller steps to make sure all details are accounted for, which allows for the big-picture vision to come first.'
- 'Hard work, discipline, and determination replace instant gratification and frivolity.'

Taking Gem Essences:

Add between two to five drops of gem essence to a glass of water, then sip at intervals throughout the day.

You can **dowse with a pendulum** to find out:

1. Which essence/s you require: Place your gem essence bottles in a group and ask whether there is a gem essence needed for today, tomorrow, the week ahead, or the upcoming month. You may find you're guided to more than one essence...
2. How many doses do you require: Ask the pendulum how many days the essence should be taken. Stick to questions

that allow for a 'yes' or 'no' answer. For instance: 'Should I take this essence once?' 'Should I take this essence twice?' and so forth.

When taking gem essences. the benefits can be reduced if you are consuming substances that alter the body's metabolism, "non-pure" and "harmful" beverages like coffee, tea, or alcohol. Also, cigarettes, pharmaceutical drugs, recreational drugs, and processed or preservative-induced foods. Chemicals inside or on your body too. Your mind, body, and spirit need to be as pure as possible to reap the benefits, which requires a pure channel. See your body as a sacred vessel, in other words, because crystals are divine and want to infuse you with sacredness! Additionally, if you are taking a homeopathic remedy or prescribed drug, it is advised that you not take gem essences until the course of treatments is complete.

2

High Vibration Techniques

Vibration Raising Techniques

Aura Protection

In my other book, *Astrology and Crystals,* you discovered what an aura is and why it's so powerful. Now, you're going to find out how to protect your aura with the help of celestial gemstones and crystals. Exciting stuff, right? This wisdom is unique, it's not generic. You won't find it in many other books because it's specialist information straight from a qualified crystal therapist. We live in more than a physical universe; infinite potential is real. There is more than the physical realm and more than the five senses. Extrasensory perception, clairvoyance, channeling abilities, healing powers, psychic phenomena, divine insights, advanced dreaming techniques, receiving messages and communication from the subtle realms of spirit, and all kinds of evolved abilities linked to spirit, light, and sound - the three pillars of our universe - are real. There are limitless possibilities available when we accept and embrace multidimensionality. As your aura is a protective bubble connecting you to the infinite, as well as the subtle realms of the mental, emotional, spiritual, astral, soul, and causal planes, where we transmit and receive messages from the divine, it's important to strengthen and protect your aura.

Pendants, necklaces, and crystals carried on your person for protection are advised. They are ideal for keeping your vibrations high, as well as keeping your aura or electromagnetic energy field free from harm and pollution. The best protective pendants and necklaces are ones relating to: the *Root chakra* and the *Third Eye chakra*. These amplify your vibrations to high levels, the Root being the cord to ancestral and earthly energies, which bring grounding, security, self-preservation, ancient wisdom, self-knowledge, passion, vitality, physical instincts for protection, stamina, and stability. And the Third Eye being a link to psychic protection, intuition, vision, prophecy, higher cerebral and spiritual gifts, and divine light and truth. The Third Eye shields and protects, as well as strengthening intuition and psychic power to see through BS, deception, and potential harm heading your way.

Amulets and Jewelry for Protection

So, here are the best crystals to use for amulets of protection, crystal pendants, and jewelry or gemstones to keep on your person:

Smoky Quartz

Smoky Quartz is a clear yellow-brown crystal connected to the Root chakra, perfect for all aspects of grounding. Smoky Quartz enhances grounding, security, and self-preservation, as well as self-alignment, boundaries, and inner strength. This gemstone is unique, as, in addition to *protection* like all other Root chakra stones, it also helps immensely with shadow work. Smoky Quartz enables you to explore and observe or ascertain your shadow, your darker or less desirable traits and attributes, and then integrate them for enlightenment or your ultimate best self. This beautiful gemstone helps you feel secure and safe in your body and physical surroundings, while uncovering BS, wounds, trauma, pain, and shadow attributes. Life force energy linking to kundalini, spiritual powers, psychic gifts, and instincts are able to travel freely from Root to Crown. This releases lots of hidden blockages while energizing wisdom and self-knowledge on the deepest levels. The more wise and self-knowledgeable you are, the more you can protect yourself from dangerous people or situations, or harmful energies.

New beginnings, pure potential, and self-mastery are part of Smoky Quartz's healing properties. It's a crystal that amplifies seeds of change, self-awareness, and gentle feminine healing energy, also being linked to personal alchemy, and making peace with your shadow self so that fresh energy and new perspectives arise. Furthermore, it is ideal for all matters of self-projection and longevity. Smoky Quartz promotes self-realization, self-actualization, and enlightenment, not through denying or rejecting shadow aspects of yourself, but through accepting and embracing them for healing, clearing, and balancing, as well as integration.

Hematite

Hematite is a second protection stone, bringing the powers of grounding, security, stability, perseverance, tenacity, inner strength, and self-knowledge. Hematite is known as the "sacred essence of Mother Earth" herself, ideal for strengthening the physical body, blood, and circulatory system. It stabilizes, cleanses, clears, aligns, and brings a solid and dependable energy; it can help you be more practical, wise, and discerning, as well as logical, empathic, and down-to-earth. Hematite connects you to a higher spiritual power while grounding your internal energy signature simultaneously. Spirituality and practicality merge and combine. It can help with feelings of "being away with the fairies" while still allowing for spiritual gifts, vision, and big-picture thinking. Subtle, psychic, and spiritual energy increase through Hematite's unique energy field, and it's excellent for the mind, body, and spirit connection! It has a strengthening, harmonizing, balancing, grounding, and stabilizing effect when held, used for protection or meditation, or worked with as an amulet or healing stone. Overall, this is a powerful protection gemstone...

Black Obsidian

Obsidian is a black crystal with white or gray markings, signifying protection, grounding, and ancient wisdom. This powerful stone brings flashes of insight and inspiration, protecting you from all sorts of harmful energies; electromagnetic harm, negative energy, psychic attack, and environmental pollution. White symbolizes purity, intuition, and faith, while gray represents sensibility, dependability, and professionalism, coupled with sophistication. Black, of course, represents strength, grounding, and psychic gifts linked to the earth - earthly energy. Obsidian is found in volcanic regions all around the world and is formed from rapidly cooled lava. It enhances inner strength, courage, and a sense of practicality and determination. It grounds, stabilizes, protects, soothes, and strengthens, while being ideal for releasing fears, amplifying your spirit, and healing deep wounds. Traumas can be transformed, repressed or hidden emotions can be brought to conscious light, and purging and cleansing occurs on a deep level. Obsidian helps with scars of the past, secrets, repressed memories, traumatic experiences pushed down to the subconscious, and emotional instability. Blocks and issues in the Root chakra can be overcome; further, explosive tendencies like rage or anger can be combated.

Black Tourmaline

Black tourmaline is a black, opaque, or slightly translucent gemstone with the powers of realignment, grounding, and soul cleansing. It brings strength, stability, physical stamina, positive changes, transformation, and purity. It awakens and revitalizes your senses, while bringing truth and clarity to your intentions. It protects you from harmful and negative energy, also cleansing your aura, combined with deflecting negative energy away from you. Black Tourmaline sparks soul remembrance, so you can find your sense of home and belonging within. It is perfect for clearing away karmic stories and toxic cycles, further providing space for the new to emerge. It's great to keep anywhere in your bedroom, in your pockets when out and about, as a pendant or necklace for protection, or on windowsills in your home. It repels negative energy at high levels and shields your auric field against psychic attack. Limitless potential, alignment with your soul's mission, and life path and purpose recognition are core to this gemstone's healing powers. Also, new beginnings, raw and unlimited creative life force, and passion projects. *Home everywhere* is increased and encouraged without losing touch of reality or sacrificing your boundaries.

GROUNDING CRYSTALS FOR PROTECTION

Sodalite

Sodalite is a powerful gemstone that will help to awaken your psychic abilities, protecting you through amplified psychological, mental, and spiritual gifts. The more you strengthen your intuitive muscle, the more you can sense deception, manipulation, and BS, as well as danger in more serious situations. It is used for the Throat and Third Eye chakras, while sparking the Higher Self. Intuition, depth, subtle perception, emotional intelligence, peace of mind, clarity, and seeing through illusions expand. Sodalite dispels negative energy, mental tension, distorted frequencies arising through confusion, and misinformation. It can bring in higher truth, wisdom, inspiration, angelic contact and guidance, and communication with the divine. It enhances self-protection and strengthens the auric field, specifically through the realms of mind, the astral and soul planes, and the spiritual body. With sea and sky colors, (light) blue and white, Sodalite symbolizes inspiration, air, angelic connection, communication, self-expression, faith, intuition, and white light. Also, it brings peace, comfort, and serenity, as well as tranquility, contemplation, introspection, self-reflection, and meditation. Its energy is calming, balancing, and clarifying, while bringing enhanced mental exchanges, communication, and self-control, which further sparks potent psychic and spiritual gifts.

Lapis Lazuli

Lapis Lazuli is an excellent gemstone for protection, psychic gifts, and advanced communication powers linked to the spirit world. It was revered (highly respected) by the ancient Egyptians for its truth-bringing and purging powers. It represents inner truth, power, purification, intuition, positive magic, cleansing, self-confidence, and manifestation. It aids friendships, protects you from negativity and psychic attack, and amplifies self-esteem, confidence, and charisma at high levels. Lapis Lazuli is a powerful dream stone too, so you can use it to connect with the subtle and spiritual powers of the universe, in addition to receiving subconscious wisdom and guidance from your Higher Self, in dreams! This strengthens your aura in waking life. The more you connect with the subtle and subconscious world of spiritual energy, the more powerful your mental, astral, and psychic gifts become.

Lapis Lazuli promotes self-knowledge, ancient wisdom, and knowledge of sacred and universal laws. Other healing properties for holistic wellbeing include self-expression, honesty, empathy, morality, and nobility, in addition to higher channeling and divine contact gifts, and grounding, wisdom and patience. Lapis Lazuli helps you take accountability, live more in alignment with your truth, and be more responsible, self-respecting, and transparent in daily affairs. It can help you pay attention to the smaller details while keeping sight of the bigger picture.

Celestite

Celestite is a clear or sky-blue transparent crystal that is ideal for connecting you to the subtle, ethereal, and spiritual realms. It is known as the stone of connecting with the angels, and brings calmness, joy, and serenity, in addition to harmony, self-alignment, self-expression, powerful visions, and prophetic and psychic gifts at high levels. It aligns you with cosmic or universal consciousness, sparks inspiration, awakens divine remembrance, and alleviates trauma, wounds, pain from loss or heartache, sadness, grief, and anger. Celestite connects you with a higher power, divine inspiration, self-realization, clairvoyance, mediumship, and potent psychic abilities for protection. It can alleviate stress, anxiety, and insecurities on minor or major levels. It puts you in touch with your soul while energizing your Higher Self. Imagination, inspiration, multidimensional awareness and communication, positive self-talk, optimism, and astral enhancement are amplified. Deep and celestial wisdom, self-knowledge, and insight are available; the energy is dreamy, contemplative, powerful, divine, spiritual, visionary, prophetic, and protective, further being one of the few crystals that connect you directly to your guides and angels, if this is what you desire.

Angelite

Angelite is ideal for mediumship and channeling, which in turn, increases protective powers tenfold. It is the perfect crystal for inner guidance, Higher Self alignment, truth, clarity, subtle perception, and spiritual powers, in addition to faith, self-realization, divine inspiration, self-actualization, and telepathy. Enhanced psychic and telepathic gifts open you to a world of multidimensionality, equally stimulating astral, soul, and spirit-body contact. Fear alchemizes into insight, stagnation transforms to growth and change, and toxic and limiting or self-sabotaging cycles can be overcome with grace, confidence, and nobility. Purity, majesty, integrity, selflessness, and modesty amplify. Angelite expands your connection to all-that-is, aligning you with the Great Spirit, powerful manifestation and creative gifts, and inner sublimity. It increases tranquility, serenity, and peace, as well as power, personal autonomy, and self-sovereignty. Angelite expands self-healing powers, astral projection, transcendental states, higher consciousness, and a need for social cohesion, order, unity, justice, and equality. Fairness and harmony can be restored, so it is ideal for all matters of personal and planetary protection (protection in your personal life, as well as any healing intentions you may carry for the wider collective). You can use Angelite for spirit journeys within and around, to connect to a greater source of personal power, self-awareness, and universal truth. Further, Angelite transmutes deep-seated pain, trauma, and fear into miracles, magic, and synchronicity!

Selenite

A final Higher Self stone for protection, amulets, and jewelry, Selenite is special due to its links with the Moon. It is named after Selene, the ancient Greek goddess of the Moon, and is transparent and white in color. This crystal is for the Crown chakra, activating consciousness and higher self-awareness, in addition to spiritual gifts, subtle energy perception, dream states, divine contact, and spirit guide, ancestor, and animal communication. It sparks transformation, change, and catalytic shifts in self and others, so for yourself and if you choose to help and heal others (being a channel...). *Fun fact*: the largest discovered crystal cave in the world is made out of Selenite crystals! Selenite clears negative energy from your aura, awakens dormant soul gifts, and protects you from psychic attack; negative energy coupled with the harmful intentions of others can be healed and released. Your auric field gets a boost, upgrade, and real cleansing and purification with Selenite, and you will find evolved avenues of wisdom and sacred knowledge flow to you. Blocks to abundance, joy, friendship, love, health, prosperity, and longevity can be soothed and eased. Creative and artistic projects get an upgrade too.

HIGHER SELF CRYSTALS FOR PROTECTION

Aquamarine

Although for the Throat chakra, Aquamarine is another one to use for protection in amulets or jewelry. This is because it is one of the best stones for emotional calmness, balance, and clarity. Aquamarine soothes emotions while balancing and harmonizing the emotional and psychological bodies. It is a beautiful and calming, yet stimulating and soul-sparking crystal simultaneously; it increases powers of protection, personal truth, and self-knowledge, in addition to sovereignty, independence, and freedom. It can break down illusory barriers and restrictions without succumbing to rebellious, immature, or ungrounded tendencies. It sparks respect, conservatism, and healthy boundaries for self-love and longevity in equal measure... Holistically, Aquamarine inspires prophetic vision, intuition, psychic instincts, wisdom, inspiration, emotional intelligence, imagination, creative genius, innovation, originality, artistic excellence, and amazing higher vibrational qualities in high measure. It's known as the *Stone of Prophets and Healers*, so it's no wonder this gem should be part of your amulet or protective jewelry collection.

Empathy, compassion, selflessness, gentleness, sensitivity, grace, universal love, devotion, service, and sincerity increase, within the parameters of having healthy boundaries. This crystal is particularly effective for HSPs (highly sensitive people) or empaths, or generally those with an overly giving and overly trusting personality. Its colors are blue-green, symbolizing tranquility, subtle perception, prophecy, clear thinking, emotional balance and intelligence, and all feminine qualities. Aquamarine is known as the Stone of Prophets, so this is essential for your path. Embodying the energy of the sea, it has strong psychic and intuitive influences, also motivating positive change, movement, and open-mindedness. Lastly, it's an excellent mood booster, stabilizer, and activator of creative and soul talents and gifts, while aligning you with higher spiritual powers. It helps with fears, insecurities, illusions, and traumas of all kinds, while putting you on track with your soul path or purpose. Remembering the divine plan in store for you can be attained and realized.

Dispelling Negative Energy

This is a technique that should only be attempted once you have become familiar with crystals and their power, in addition to increasing your own vibration. Dispelling negative energy is similar to a unique *Shamanic technique* known as *extraction*. A shamanic practitioner "draws" negative energy, pain, or trauma out of the recipient, using their left hand to pull it out and their right hand to send healing light and energy. The negative energy then goes into the ether, where spiritual guides and helpers pass it on to Spirit. Why share this with you? Because dispelling negative energy is something you can do yourself. All you need to do is keep up a regular meditation practice, keep your vibration relatively high through good diet, prayer, and spiritual practices, and make sure you have some mode of protection in place.

Dispelling is literally drawing negative or harmful energy out and clearing it away. This can be performed with either a **Clear Quartz** or **Selenite** crystal, preferably one shaped like a wand. Some others can be used, such as Malachite and other Third Eye and Crown chakra crystals.

To begin, you should first perform some centering, grounding, or vibration-raising activity, or all three if you're feeling ambitious. Dispelling is very effective at clearing the aura and etheric field, as well as healing (unblocking) negative energy from the chakras. To begin, create a connection with your crystal. This can be done through meditation or through simply closing your eyes and setting your intention. Hold your crystal in your left palm with your right hand over the top, like in the *Universal Flow Meditation*. Take 3- 5 deep breaths and speak or project some intentions into your crystal, like "Thank you for your healing energy" or "I open up to your healing power." Or "I charge you with love and light." As your right hand is the giving hand and your left is the receiving, hold the crystal in your left hand with the point facing outwards. You don't need to grip too tightly, just comfortably, and with intention. Sit down in a meditative position and point the crystal towards one of your energy centers you feel has become blocked or polluted with other people's energy, harmful thoughts, or detrimental judgements.

We tend to pick up on illusions, other people's delusions and false judgements of us, because we are social creatures. Even the most non-empathic person is capable of empathy, and this means we are sensitive to the thoughts and speech of others. In this respect, it's very easy to become "bogged down," polluted by false stories, projections, and circulated wounds and trauma. It is likely, therefore, that you will feel drawn to use this dispelling technique on your Sacral chakra, as this is the center of interpersonal relationships, emotions, sensuality, social bonds, and sexuality. We accumulate good and bad karma in our Sacral chakra from our youth and past lives, due to us growing through cycles of immaturity (centered around emotions, friendships, and so forth). Other areas that usually accumulate psychic debris are the Third Eye and Crown chakras, due to the fact that we are, holistically speaking, a spiritually disconnected global society. Keep this in mind when considering the dispelling technique for your own healing path.

Once you've chosen or felt the area that needs some cleansing and good energy, point the end of the crystal towards it, holding your right arm straight by your side with your palm flat facing outwards, as if you were imitating a dance, yogic, or freedom pose. The key is to have the palm of your right hand facing *upwards* and *away from you*. With your intention, draw out the negative or blocked energy. Visualize a stream of pure golden light physically drawing out the energy, while combining it with conscious breathing. Be strong in your mind and your intention; use subtle force, not an over-exertion of force. Let's repeat this. Force is necessary, but it should be gentle power. Reflect on the duality symbol.

The duality symbol: yin, darkness, femininity, passivity,

*receptivity, and subconsciousness, and yang, light,
masculinity, action, force, and consciousness. There is an
eternal dance of opposing forces that equally complement
each other. The yin and yang duality symbol is the perfect
ideal to embody and practice in your spiritual healing
endeavors.*

Once you begin to feel a tingling sensation or a shift occurring in your chakra, crystal, and left hand, send an intention to your *right hand*. Create the circuit in your mind, from the golden light drawing out the harmful energy; it travels through the crystal, into your left hand, and straight out into your right. It should not stay in your body; you are merely a channel and do not wish to hold onto this energy. Send it straight to your right hand and watch it dispel into the ether around you. This should be done for 2- 3 minutes. At this stage, you may feel intuitively that you want to do a few gently forceful and abrupt arm jolts or move your hand outwards in a flowing motion. Your intuition should tell you what to do, as long as you have spent sufficient time working with crystals beforehand.

Remember to end with setting an intention, closing the current. You should cleanse and recharge your crystal after this and perform some grounding and centering activities on yourself. You may even want to "spark" your palms together to close the circuit.

Third Eye Strengthening

This exercise is simple yet highly effective. It strengthens your mental abilities and shields you from psychic attack. It amplifies your aura and sparks soul remembrance. You will start to remember your destiny and life purpose on a deep level. You can reflect on your past, access past life memories, and contemplate the mind, body, and spirit connection. Awareness of your future self, your Higher Self, can be shown... Compassion, self-love, intuition, confidence, and self-alignment increase. Strengthening your aura through daily or weekly minor or longer practices such as this will enhance your inner chi. Chi is essential life force, responsible for all sorts of psychic and evolved gifts, so do not underestimate the power of this exercise.

Your Third Eye is a bridge, a cord. It opens you up to psychic perception and spiritual phenomena, in addition to the spiritual-quantum world, where crystals work their magic. The following exercise is best performed with **Amethyst, Lapis Lazuli, Azurite, Sodalite, Celestite, Angelite,** *or* **Clear Quartz.**

1. Begin by getting into your meditative space, taking deep breaths, and centering yourself through coming into your body; the first steps to any meditation or visualization exercise.
2. Mentally construct a protective pyramid around yourself. The pyramid is symbolic of the three, the holy trinity; the pyramids of Giza were created based on ancient knowledge regarding sacred geometry, as were other temple pyramids around the world. Just as colors carry a unique frequency, so do shapes; shapes are the building blocks of life. The key to this exercise is to combine visualization, inner knowing, and intuition with trust and faith, as well as knowledge of the multidimensional and transcendental state of things.
3. Once you are in your calm and peaceful space (within), bring your chosen crystal up to your Third Eye. Lightly tap it against the center of your forehead a few times. Swirl it round in a circular motion, feeling the crystal's energy interacting with yours.
4. Visualize healing energy sparking from the crystal. Repeat the process up to 10 times, beginning with light tapping and then gentle rubbing... Feel yourself connect to it on an energetic level. Tap into its healing properties on an energetic level.
5. You can program and project intentions into the crystal whilst rubbing it against your Third Eye. This is the next step. Essentially, you are activating your psychic center through the stimulation and connection with the crystal, combined with your intentions and receptivity to its gifts.
6. Finally, picture yourself inside a pyramid. See yourself inside a pyramid similar to the largest pyramid of Giza, in Egypt, or

another if you're familiar with other sacred sites around the world.

7. You can ask for guidance, divine inspiration, or wisdom from the spiritual and subtle planes to come through. Set an intention for your best path, ultimate self, and Higher Self healing. Stay in this energetic grid or chamber for as long as it feels right; the more you increase your inner light, the more strength, nobility, wisdom, power, and intuitive force you will have access to.

This exercise is amazing for connecting you to subconscious knowledge and wisdom that has been repressed or "pushed down." Activating your Third Eye with the help of crystals sparks forgotten or momentarily suppressed knowledge to shine through. The unconscious becomes conscious. Memories, past life memories, and visions can come through, as your Third Eye is a bridge or portal to super-consciousness.

A Tree Grounding Meditation

This *Tree Meditation* for grounding and centering is incredibly powerful. Here is some secret knowledge for you:

1. The roots of the tree symbolize your feet.
2. The trunk is equivalent to your spine.
3. The leaves correspond with your Crown.

Begin by finding a quiet or comfortable place outside. Choose a tree that resonates with you, one you feel drawn to. Use your intuition and trust your instincts! Sit down with your knees bent, feet flat on the earth, and back straight against the trunk of the tree. Gently rest against the tree's trunk, and take some deep breaths. Release tension and negative feelings, just become present. Start to feel universal life force energy flowing through you in unison with the tree. Your feet should be at one with the earth, which means shoes and socks off. Did you know your hands and feet have chakras too? Now you do. These are known as palm chakras.

Place a Quartz crystal in front of your feet, directly on the earth. Hold another Quartz crystal in the palm of your hands with your hands cupped. These gemstones should already be cleansed, charged, and programmed (intentions set). You can equally use more crystals and get creative, such as placing seven around you, symbolizing the seven chakras, or creating a crystal grid of Clear Quartz and/or other Higher Self enhancing crystals.

1. Start with 10- 12 conscious breaths, close your eyes, and bring your awareness inside. Once you feel centered, begin to visualize a loving gentle golden light traveling through your feet, up your spine, and to the top of your head.
2. Breathe slowly and deeply. With each breath, visualize this loving light - healing life force - traveling through you. Meditate on the energy similarities as you breathe, like how your feet are linked to the earth, how your spine is like the tree's trunk, and how your Crown is deeply similar to the top of the tree... The tree's leaves serve as ethereal cords to the infinite, the divine, and the Great Unknown.
3. Repeat this beautiful synergy visualization 10- 15 times, starting at your feet and ending in your Crown connecting to the ether. Once you feel a steady flow, reverse the process; begin at the top of your head, your Crown, make your way

down your spine, and end in your feet. Visualize the healing light flowing through you, while being aware of your connection to the tree.

4. Sit with any sensations wishing to arise for a little while. Become conscious of the earth beneath you, the elements around you, and so forth. Then, once you have begun to feel the tree's heartbeat as if it's your own, which you will do, repeat the meditation but with the following additions:

5. Visualize loving life force energy and healing light flowing into the roots of the tree, up its trunk, and spilling into the leaves and ether-astral cords, surrounding it. You will still be connected to all the sensations of your physical body, but you will start to see the energy moving through the tree (instead of through you, as was the case in part 1). Perform this 10- 15 times.

6. Again, reverse the process: visualize beautiful golden healing light coming in through the ether, the energetic cords of the tree's leaves, traveling down its spine (trunk) and into the earth or roots below.

7. At this stage, you should feel completely at one with the tree, totally connected and in divine flow. The tree's roots are your feet, the trunk is your spine and kundalini, and the leaves are your Crown! The feeling cannot be described in words, yet it is very real...

8. About 10- 15 minutes into the meditation, you may have a powerful awakening, a deep sense of remembrance. You will sense the ancient and majestic tree as if you are it, entwined through an energetic-spiritual world.

9. Once you get familiar with this, maintaining steady breathing and experiencing sensations of deep peace and safety (remember you will be in nature, perhaps in a public space), you can then add stage three to the meditation: Visualize the loving golden healing light flowing through both of you simultaneously. Your roots/feet, trunk/spine, and leaves/Crown.... You and the tree are *one and the same*, your energy fields have merged. You are bonded on a deep and telepathic level. It's a beautiful and powerful connection.

Trees are ancient, mighty, and strong; they have deep roots, and a majestic essence that connects their sustaining energy to the ether. Through their roots, they receive powerful healing energy and light to help us achieve longevity, balance, and good health. Simultaneously, their "Crown" is their leaves, subtle threads that connect them to the ether, spiritual world, and soul and causal planes. If you perform this tree meditation regularly, you will begin to feel just how safe, supported, and cherished you are by the physical world, as well as perhaps spirit guides, animals or ancestors unique to you. If you are someone who works with elemental energy or angels and Archangels, you can call on their guidance at the end of the meditation. This is an extra part that can enhance your experience tenfold.

You may even feel a strong swirl of energy emanating from your back, as if the tree is *communicating* with you. Remember, we are all connected. You and the tree are one, so you can receive potent messages, life force, and inspirational qualities that connect you to spiritual healing gifts and powers, in addition to potent knowledge from the crystal realm. Your soul awakens, your Higher Self sparks, and you become more magnificent in your personal power, inner strength, and integrity...

Eventually, you will feel a spiraling circular motion, and will start to feel the tree's heartbeat as if it's your own. Once you get familiar with this, you can expand the meditation as long or as deep as you wish. You can ask for divine guidance from your Higher Self, spiritual wisdom from your guides or ancestors, or messages that can enhance your path from your angels or Archangels.

Part 4:

A final part of the meditation, which should only be performed once you have found a steady sync and got into a groove, become familiar and comfortable with the other parts, etc, is to add Third Eye activation exercises to the end. You can do this by taking one of your crystals and holding it up to your Third Eye. In such a deep and soul aligned space, *mystical and multidimensional* encounters are possible, which means powerful revelations and divine insights from the crystal king and queendoms. You can activate your Merkabah, connect to your light body, or speak to spirit guides and subtle life forms, like angels, personal spirit animals, elementals, or the Great Spirit itself.

Earthing

Here are some ideas to develop a deep connection, also grounding you and awakening your Higher Self simultaneously:

- Walking barefoot on the ground with a crystal for protection on your being... Walking barefoot increases your connection with Mother Earth, which expands ancestral earthly energies and celestial higher energies simultaneously. This allows for a perpetual flow of yin and yang, balanced and unified currents for wholeness and harmony!
- Taking your gemstones out with you when visiting national parks, forests, lakes, oceans, local parks, or nature reserves... Keeping crystals on your person is ideal for your healing path because it keeps you energized, aligned, and spiritually aware.

- Burying crystals in the earth... This is the 'grounding' technique. It's highly advised, particularly for Root and Heart chakra gemstones.
- Placing your gemstones near medicinal herbs and plants or trees to absorb their energy... Placing your crystals on houseplants to help the houseplants grow quicker and better... You can keep gemstones and sacred crystals on your houseplants to increase their glow and growing capacity. It's true; gemstones amplify plant auras just as much as they expand ours.
- Combining crystal water/gem essences with flower essences and herbal remedies... This is a topic you will need to delve into on your own (Google research, anyone?!) There are lots of specific gem essence/water and flower or herbal essence remedy combinations to experiment with. Both complement each other, as both hold high life force.

Increasing Chi: Channeling Abilities

Many people around the world are waking up to the healing power of crystals. They are subsequently waking up to their own healing power and ability to channel light energy or chi. Chi is the universal life force that flows through every living thing. It's been given many names, such as reiki, prana, ki, or source energy. In many practices and schools of thought, such as Taoist philosophy and healing systems like Reiki, disease is believed to originate in the etheric body, and subsequently manifest in the physical. This means that all mental, emotional, and physical illnesses, pains, and imbalances originate on a subtler plane of existence. As crystals remove blockages, release trapped energy, and activate consciousness, working with crystals to increase inner chi flow can change your vibration. You are aware that both we humans and the crystal king/queendom have an electromagnetic energy field. You are also knowledgeable about the fact that crystals interact and heal through the subtle bodies and planes, the etheric blueprint, astral body, aura, and so forth. Channeling is connecting to a higher power, and there are many ways to do this. Fasting, detoxification, diet changes, tai chi, qi gong, other spiritual and gentler martial arts, daily meditation, yoga, nature walks, music or art therapy, and self-therapy are all perfect methods to increase chi flow. So is *creating a chi ball*.

Chi Balls: A Powerful Way to Spark Your Best Self

Chi balls are exactly what they sound like; balls of chi or universal healing life force. Chi balls can be created in any time or place, and are powerful for increasing psychic gifts, enhancing self-awareness, releasing blocks, and easing discomfort, tension, and stress or trauma on any of the planes. Chi balls move energy up to your Third Eye and Crown, your higher energy centers, while removing blocks holding you back. It's very simple and easy to do, and great for both beginners and those more advanced in crystal healing and energy work alike. A chi ball is something you can create in any time or place, like at home with intention, such as in a meditation to activate psychic gifts, or when out and about. When out and about, you can create a chi ball to heal yourself, moving trapped or blocked energy to spark important qualities, and overcome social anxiety or fears and insecurities. For example, creating a chi ball for your Third Eye will stimulate vision, intuition, subtle perception, psychic powers, and spiritual abilities. Additionally, peace of mind, calmness, clarity, peace, higher perspectives, and tranquility. A chi ball for the Third Eye eases stress, tension, and mental distortion, helping to release clouded judgments or muddied perception. It's also great to help against psychic attack and other people's negativities!

A chi ball for the Heart is perfect if you need to re-spark or increase empathy, compassion, universal love, self-love, tolerance, patience, and gentleness, moreover grace, generosity, selflessness, and virtually all the Heart chakra qualities. You can create a chi ball for your Sacral chakra to increase energy flow to your capacity to relate to others. The Sacral chakra symbolizes interpersonal relationships, friendships, creativity, joy, self-empowerment relating to social connections, and emotions, as well as vulnerability, openness, warmth, sensuality, sexual life force, and romance. It is often referred to as the *creativity-sexuality-emotional* center, because it is where these three significant themes tie in. Each sparks the others, and when there are blocks here or no life force flow, each is negatively impacted.

I've included the Sacral, Heart, and Third Eye chakras, as these are where blocks linked to romance, friendship, and sociability often originate. You can, of course, create a chi ball for your Root chakra to activate security, grounding, and belonging, your Solar Plexus for ambition, self-empowerment, and optimism, your Throat for self-expression and communication, and your Crown for cosmic consciousness, faith, purity, and divine or angelic contact (if you want to go really high into the spirit realms). Chi flows through your body like energy flows through a circuit. Your left hand or palm chakra is known as the "receiver;" your right hand or palm gives, it's known as the "giver of energy." *(Please note when channeling energy to heal others both hands fulfill the same role, but this is a whole other topic.)* I repeat: for a chi ball to heal yourself, left is receiving and right is giving. To make a chi ball, you have to come to terms with the reality of there being invisible, subtle, and spiritual energy present in our physical universe. You place your hands in a cupping motion and visualize healing light growing in between them. It's this simple! Yet deeply powerful.

Assuming you want to develop and practice this over time, here is the more carefully planned out way to create and receive the benefits of a chi ball. You can, of course, make one anywhere. You may want to put on some healing and "vibration raising" music, such as nature sounds, Tibetan singing bowls or bells and chimes, and binaural beats, or shamanic or tribal drumming or OM chanting. For binaural beats, 432 Hz and 528 Hz are perfect frequencies to play. 432 Hz is the resonance sound of the harmony of the earth and universe, also known as the "Gaia frequency," while 528 Hz is known as the "love frequency."

How to make a chi ball:

1. Find a quiet spot where you won't be disturbed or where you feel comfortable, get into a meditative space, and take some deep breaths. Set your intention to finding silence and peace within, and make sure your breathing is steady.
2. Bring your hands up to the level of your heart chakra. Make a cupping motion, your palms should be facing each other, an inch or two apart. If you're already an experienced energy healer, like a Reiki practitioner, you may find your hands naturally begin a few inches apart. This is because of the purpose of the chi ball; chi grows and expands within your hands...
3. Start to breathe deeply, while projecting your intention into the ball of beautiful healing energy growing in between your hands and palm chakras. Project the intentions of stillness of mind, also remembering how chi - universal healing energy and spiritual life force - flows through all living things. It's abundant, infinite, and always available.
4. The color of the light should be pure white or golden. If you're making one for a specific chakra, you can visualize a mixture of white-golden light and the chakra color. So, red for your Root, orange for your Sacral, yellow for your Solar Plexus, green for your Heart, blue for your Throat, purple or indigo for your Third Eye, and white for your Crown. With each inhale, picture the beautiful healing light and energy growing and expanding within your hands. With each exhale, see this coming out of your palms and 'energizing' the life force inside your hands. Form a cyclic motion and powerful visual imagery.

5. This exercise can be performed for as little as five minutes and up to one hour, however long feels comfortable and right for you. The average amount of time I would suggest energizing your chi ball is 10- 15 minutes. But start out shorter and work your way up with deeper practice and experience.

6. Once your hands have started to feel a sufficient gravitational pull, i.e. they have moved further apart, due to the built-up ball of energy growing inside them, you will actually be able to feel your chi ball circulating around... It's a euphoric and blissful experience. Slowly bring the ball up to your chosen area.

7. Finally, once you feel ready, "pour" the energy into or onto your chosen chakra. Watch it spill and flow into you, filling you with light, love, and healing gifts from Spirit. Visualize it, feel it happening at the same time. Leave it there for a few minutes, until you feel the desired intentions.

8. To conclude, gently rest the palms of your hands over the chakra with your left palm flat first, and your right hand over the top. Keep your hands there for a few moments while feeling the warmth of healing light flowing through you. At this stage, you can say thank you - the act of gratitude amplifies the experience and positive energy flow more... To finish, rub your hands together a few times as if you are sparking them against one another, attempting to light a fire. End by bringing your hands down onto your knees in a meditative position.

If you start to feel chi balls are your go-to and really work at activating self-healing gifts, you can start to experiment with something known as "chakra linking." This is where you make a chi ball for each of two chakras and "link" them after both have been created. These are the best combinations for *chakra healing*:

- Root and Heart
- Sacral and Throat
- Solar Plexus and Third Eye
- Heart and Crown

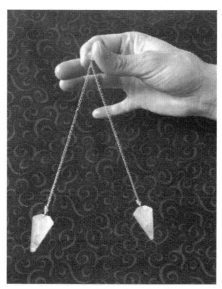

Divination: Pendulum Dowsing

Divination or pendulum dowsing is an integral aspect of healing with crystals. Pendulum dowsing is connecting to the subconscious and ether around you. It involves, firstly, becoming mindful and conscious of subtle energy, i.e. how everything is interconnected, as well as how there is an invisible energy connecting all things. Secondly, it's connecting to your higher mind or Higher Self for clear wisdom and guidance to shine through. Then, thirdly, it involves being completely faithful to the existence and presence of spirit, of spiritual energy and universal life force.

Pendulums give you a 'yes' or 'no' answer through their gravitational pull. First, you must align, center, and take some deep breaths. Get your breathing steady. Harmonize and synchronize your breath and inner state to the spiritual or energetic world around you. Remember, there is a quantum field and powerful ethereal dimension connecting you, the crystal, and everything else. Make sure your crystal pendulum is cleansed and purified - charged or programmed. Always keep your crystal pendulum in a clear space, such as on an altar or shrine, or in an area of your bedroom you treat sacredly. Sacredness and purity are two key components to divination. Pendulum dowsing is a ceremonial ritual, of sorts; all rooted in light and goodness, of course! (There's nothing dark or evil and satanic about crystals...)

Ceremonial ritual can be as light or deep as you want it to be. Some people treat crystal healing lightly, whilst others see it as something a bit more deep and mystical. Both are real, both can be true. It's all about vibration and energy, what works for you, and what intended results you wish to see. For instance, you can ask a question lightly and receive an answer within seconds, or you could perform an hour-long meditation complete with sage, fasting, and intense chakra alignment to ask your pendulum an important life question. *Hint*: your astrological Sun, Moon, and Rising signs might have something to do with this... ;)

Pendulums are crystals or gemstones suspended on a string or chain. They work on the mental, emotional, spiritual, and astral planes, and activate the subconscious mind too. Using a crystal pendulum is very easy, but you must have the following: **belief, inner knowing (trust, faith in the divine and Great Spirit), and intention**.

Questions *must* be yes or no-related, such as 'Will I find new love soon?' 'Am I soon going to be able to travel?' 'Will I shortly be receiving a new client?' The pendulum can only offer you two answers; yes, which is shown by a clockwise spin, or no, reflected through an anti-clockwise turn. Pendulums are influenced by unseen forces. They are bound by quantum and spiritual laws, which includes a unique electromagnetic energy field pull and spin. Questions spark an innate knowing in your cells, which is connected to your past, subconscious wisdom stored, truths left untold, desires forgotten or put on hold, and everything "below the surface." Your past, present, and future selves and linked wisdom shine through in pendulum dowsing. Your subconscious coupled with your Higher Self "speak" to you. All the various emotions, beliefs, thoughts, intentions, stories, and realities you've created or chosen in this lifetime swirl around in an energetic dance or force, coming straight from and through your aura. Your auric field communicates with the pendulum. It sounds complex, but in reality, is very simple. The crystal "knows," it speaks to you; it's connected to your soul's blueprint, the entire and holistic version of yourself. Every detail is picked up on, as long as it's relevant to your question. The crystal pendulum responds directly to your auric field, all energy currents included.

Yes = clockwise
No = anti-clockwise

A minor technicality:

Pendulum dowsing should begin with asking your crystal to show you which direction is yes and which is no. Usually, yes is clockwise and no is anti-clockwise, but this is not always the case (according to crystal therapists). For the most accurate results, start by centering and grounding your energy, then create a mental connection and cord to the crystal pendulum. Then, ask which direction is yes and which is no.

Benefits of Pendulum Dowsing:

- Crystal pendulums can be used to bring insight and guidance to any aspect in life, including relationships, friendships, career choices and goals, love, health, personal projects, fitness or diet queries, creativity, life path, and any other area you wish to discover.
- They help to develop your connection to the natural world, as well as increase your ability to perceive subtle energy and receive subconscious wisdom and guidance directly from the ether.
- They raise your vibration, expand your consciousness, awaken your higher mind, stimulate intuition, and increase spiritual powers of knowing, instinct, and inner guidance.
- They can stimulate amazing creative, innovative, artistic, imaginative, and intellectual gifts, while increasing sensuality, modesty, integrity, empathy, and virtually any quality or strength required.

You might want to choose to smudge your pendulum with sage, palo santo, incense, resins like frankincense or other

herbal smudge sticks. You can cleanse and activate your crystal pendulum with music, like the universal 'OM' sound (chanting) or Tibetan bells, bowls, and chimes, or nature sounds...

Sound, Smoke, and Salt (Cleansing Methods)

There are more methods for crystal purification than cleansing, charging, grounding, and programming. These include smoke or smudging, sound, and salt. Let's get into it.

Sound

Crystals can be cleansed, charged, and activated through sound frequencies. Just as our thoughts and the power of our minds can be harnessed to program and set up our crystals for success, sound essentially activates crystals in a unique way. This is due to everything in the universe existing in a state of vibration and frequency. Scientists have discovered that objects can be moved with high-frequency acoustic vibrations, otherwise known as sound waves, and have thus learned how to make things levitate. Acoustic levitation is a real thing. As gemstones have been formed through high-vibrational frequencies projected and emitted from space, they are no different.

1. *Nature sounds*: These are specifically beneficial for grounding and earth-connecting stones, as well as celestial higher-minded gemstones. All major chakras, the Root, Sacral, Solar Plexus, Heart, Throat, Third Eye, and Crown chakra crystals are great for nature sounds. Nature sounds can include birds singing, rainforest sounds, ocean waves, rain, and gently running water. Whale and dolphin sounds or

singing are particularly melodic and tranquil. *You can find a huge array of free nature sound healing videos on YouTube.*

2. **Binaural beats**: Binaural beats are unique sound waves embodying a range of different effects, based on their frequencies. Each frequency range has a specific set of healing qualities. The frequency ranges are: Delta, 0.1- 4 Hz (deep sleep, pain relief, and healing), Theta, 4- 8 Hz (REM sleep, deep relaxation, meditation, and creativity), Alpha, 8- 13 Hz (relaxed focus, stress release, positive thinking, and fast learning), Beta, 13- 30 Hz (problem-solving, cognitive thinking, and focused attention), and Gamma, 30 Hz + (high-level cognition, memory recall, peak awareness, and transcendental states). *Again, you can find lots of free binaural beats meditation music on YouTube.*

3. **Crystal singing bowls, Tibetan singing bowls, and tuning forks:** These instruments can be purchased to supercharge your crystals. Playing Clear Quartz in a singing bowl, for example, would amplify and energize the already present metaphysical properties, like purity, intuition, and inspiration. The healing energy of each crystal gets a "boost!"

4. *Drumming*: The universal heartbeat, tribal or shamanic drumming is an excellent sound healing tool. Drumming serves as a heartbeat, making it both ancestral & primal and celestial & higher consciousness sparking. Drumming sparks higher consciousness, spiritual perspectives, and intuitive and psychic gifts at high levels. It also increases vital life force flow, ancestral powers, and grounding on deep levels. Drumming is a wonderful tool for connecting to ancient wisdom, self-healing abilities, and innate powers that can spark growth.

Smoke and Smudging

Air and ether tools include smoke, sage, and smudging, and these are highly effective. You can cleanse and clear psychic impurities and distortions that build up in your crystal's energy field through sage, smudging with herbal bundles, pure herbal incense, palo santo, or resins like frankincense. Smoke or smudging is amazingly effective and works on both the physical earthly realm and the astral and ethereal dimensions. Unwanted, harmful, and lingering negative energies are removed and purified. This is perfect for all crystals and specifically for those with a low Mohs ranking (that can't be cleansed in water).

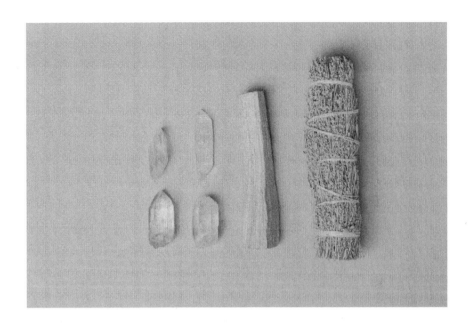

Salt (Earth)

Himalayan rock crystals, rock salt, and sea salt crystals can all be used to cleanse and purify your gemstones. (Don't use table salt! It's simply not effective.) This is a great method for crystals that can't be placed in water, i.e., those with a low Mohs rating. But all crystals can be "earthed," aka left in salt. Salt as a form of cleansing helps to release any etheric and astral impurities accumulated in your crystal's auric field. Simply leaving your crystal in a small bowl of these salts for 12-24 hours will neutralize, activate, and purify. It is a charging and grounding method, in addition to being an energizing and awakening one.

3

Crystal Meditations

'Universal Flow' Crystal Meditation

Start by placing your chosen crystal on your left hand with your palm face-up but flat. Place your right hand over the top, a few centimeters away. This meditation is all about *giving and receiving* energy.

Your *left* hand is known as your *receiving* hand.

Your *right* hand is known as your *giving* hand.

So, placing your chosen crystal on your left palm will allow you to receive its healing energies, while simultaneously giving, or letting energy flow through, with your right. This allows you to receive healing energy and also amplify your own natural healing powers, because the more you act as a channel, the more you increase your own healing abilities.

Take a few deep breaths, close your eyes, and go within; center yourself. Set your intention, thank the crystal in whichever way feels right for you. Perform a short blessing. Next, visualize a beautiful golden light drawn in through your Crown, located at the top of your head. See this flow directly into the crystal through the top of your right hand. Take your time, breath steadily, and release all fear and anxiety or insecurity. With each breath, visualize and feel this loving healing light pouring through your Crown, radiating into the crystal. It's charging it.

Continue to breathe and visualize, breathe and visualize. *Do this for anything up to 10 minutes.*

Eventually, you may find you enter a transcendental state. Also, depending on the crystal or gemstone, you may begin to receive visions, insights, or direct wisdom through your Higher Self or the ether. Once you feel the crystal is charged enough, you can either reverse your intentions, taking in the healing light and wisdom of the gemstone, or place it on your altar or shrine. You can keep the crystal for future healing endeavors or receive its healing energy in this moment.

This is a foundation for all other energy work and crystal healing endeavors to expand from. You can use this as a base for deeper and more advanced practices, further adding different elements and dimensions via expanded exercises and techniques!

Crystal Visualization Meditation

Steps 1 and 2 can be performed together as part of one meditation, or separately at different times.

Visualization Meditation:

- Create a sacred space. This can involve using incense, resin, palo santo, sage, or other cleansing and clearing herbs or plants. Also, sounds (healing music), minimal lighting, and a purified room are advised. Become present and mindful of your body and surroundings, and create a comfortable space within and around you. Meditate on the mind, body, and spirit connection for a few moments.
- Next, close your eyes and engage in some conscious breathing. You will want to feel peaceful and calm within, in order to truly feel the effects of the meditation. You should be able to feel your heart beating softly if you're already in a serene or calm space, or powerfully if there are things you know you need to let go of - ask the angels or your spirit guides for healing and release. You may feel a warm glow from your heart...
- The first stage is to synchronize your breathing to your heart. The Heart space or chakra is where spiritual beings enter into your energy field, communicate with you, and send you benevolent guidance. Without an active heart, you wouldn't be able to receive Higher Self guidance or access your higher mind, intuitive powers, and so forth.
- Place your hands over your heart, remembering that it is not just your physical heart that is affected, but also your Heart chakra, the energetic portal or wheel responsible for feelings of compassion, empathy, and self-love, as well as tolerance, patience, understanding, emotional maturity, ancient wisdom, and sensitivity.
- Place your hands over your heart, around 2- 5 inches away. This creates a current, and combined with the power of your

intentions, you can begin to synchronize your breathing to the sensations within; blood flow, life force, etc.

Step 1: Release, transmutation, and letting go

- Now your hands are in place and your breathing is at a steady and peaceful pace, picture something in your mind's eye. Visualize something you may wish to release. This is something you wish to let go of; it may be a painful memory, a traumatic experience, or repressed or blocked emotions. It could be family trauma, loss, or the pains of heartache or rejection. It might be a fear, a long-standing insecurity, or an imbalance or health ailment. The angels, your spirit team, and your Higher Self want to speak through the crystal! Benevolent forces wish to transmute any pain or traumatic memory you're holding onto. Such pains, blocks, or distortions leave you through the ether and spirit realms, merging with the divine, where they are released straight back to the Source.
- The first part of the meditation is to release, so you will be focusing all of your energy on healing, clearing, and releasing. Continue to hold the vision of your best self, your future self, and your Higher Self. Project your intentions for healing and self-alignment, continuing the visualization of light and inner self-mastery. You can stay in this energetic space for 10-15 minutes if you're starting out, or 30-45 minutes if you're more experienced. The key is to be receptive to help, while projecting the visualization of release and letting go. *Allow benevolent powers of good and healing to transmute and remove all that no longer serves. Remember to say 'thank you' at the end, blessing the experience, and sending your gratitude.*

Step 2: Integration, embodiment, and expansion

- Ask for what you want to integrate or receive, be it a quality, strength, or insight. Wisdom, higher guidance, repressed memories, self-knowledge, blessings, and protection all come into the latter. For the first two, set an intention for a specific skill or set of abilities and characteristics for integration. This meditation is all about *embodiment and expansion.*
- Now hold that intention strongly in your mind's eye. See it, feel it, and become it. Recognize that, on the spiritual and astral planes, there is an infinite source of wisdom and abundance available - there are no limitations or boundaries. The only limits and barriers are what your mind creates.
- Once you've chosen your quality or chakra area of focus, start to visualize the corresponding light. For example, if you've chosen to focus on a quality or set of characteristics related to the Root, visualize a loving red light; for the Sacral, orange; for the Solar Plexus, yellow or golden-yellow; for the Heart, green; for the Throat, sea or sky blue or royal blue; for the Third Eye, purple; and, for the Crown, white, violet, or gold.
- See it swirling through and over you, filling you with light and loving energy. Continue to project the intentions of what you want to embody, and slowly but steadily - in synchronization with your heartbeat - feel the energy swirling within your chakra(s).
- This meditation can be performed for 10-15 minutes if you're a beginner or up to 45 minutes if more advanced. Remember to alternate between yin and yang, receptivity and action, gentleness and force, and surrender/flow and intention. Always set your intention while feeling the flow of energy within you, and then follow it with a period of stillness. Yin flows into yang... yang flows into yin. You should develop a balance between receptivity and action to make the most of this.

Action (yang) enables intentions to work their magic; the healing light and crystal qualities flow into you through clear intentions and a bit of force... Receptivity (yin) allows you to receive, to be still, silent, and in a state of flow and surrender... Both are necessary.

ESSENTIAL ADVICE:

Always keep the crystal in front of you *or* in the palms of your hands. If you want to meditate in a lotus position with your hands resting on your knees, performing mudras (image for clarity below), you should have the crystal in front of you. If you would rather sit with your hands cupped, make sure your left hand is below with the right hand on top, and the crystal resting on the top of your right hand.

Here are two primary meditation positions:

'Mudra position,' crystal in front of you on the ground.

'Monk position,' crystal cupped in hands.

You can expand this meditation for angelic and spirit guide contact or communication with the following visualization. This is an extra component or dimension for you to amplify your psychic, intuitive, and healing gifts.

Visualize Your Future Self

- From the space created, picture your future self. Hold an image of your dream life or ideal self strongly in your mind's eye. See how you look, where you're situated, the environment and objects or people around you... See light shining out of your eyes, pure white light. Fill the scene with light. Envision yourself in an ethereal bubble of golden or white light; watch it pour into your auric field, flowing through your entire vessel. Meditate on purity, self-alignment, and awakening.
- Become conscious of the energetic bubble surrounding you, projecting a strong intention of purity and divinity flowing into your auric field. In this day and age, the Crown chakra is

often the missing link. This signifies that we may start to awaken our other energetic bodies or chakras, but our sense of spiritual enlightenment, faith, and absolute trust is missing. We're disconnected from the divine and super-conscious realms and dimensions.

- So, picture your future self in your ideal form. Fill the scene with light, and set an intention. Ask the universe for what you want: tell the universe what you desire. Make the intention spiritual, not rooted in some material need or thing. For instance, set an intention for happiness, longevity, true love, abundance, or security.
- Stay connected to this visual for a while, feeling your aura expanding and energy increasing the more vivid the image becomes.
- From this energetic space, you can: connect to your inner diamond light, ask for guidance from your Akashic Records, activate your Merkabah, increase/energize any quality you choose, and release past baggage or pain. The world is your oyster, so to speak, because you are a shell. You are a divine vessel waiting to be filled with light and consciousness; what are you choosing to fill yourself with?
- Set an intention for your legacy to be made known. Envision your life path, soul's purpose, and destiny. Your soul's plan wants to trickle through the subtle planes of consciousness, therefore allow it. Be open, and remember: in any given moment, there is a choice between love and fear. Fear closes you off to limited potential, new possibilities, and beautiful abundance, friendship, and true happiness. Love connects you, sparking unity, soul alignment, and an infinite number of miraculous manifestations.

To end the meditation, bring your hands down gently to your knees. Let them sit, with your palms relaxed and facing upwards/outwards, feeling the new surge of life force energy surrounding you. Be open to astral visions regarding your life's purpose and future self. You can incorporate mantras, mudras, or transcendental meditation techniques into this meditation, if you wish. Working with *Third Eye* chakra crystals can help you expand this.

Crystal Chakra Meditations

This meditation can be performed to ease blocks and release trapped energy, as well as activating the chakras. You can use Clear Quartz for each chakra, as this crystal is for kundalini energy. Or you can use a crystal for a corresponding chakra. You can also sense which of your chakras may need work, if any, through pendulum dowsing. In addition, you can ascertain which specific crystal to use for each chakra if you have a large collection.

Like in meditation 1, begin by holding your crystal on the top of your left palm with your right hand over it. Set your intentions, bless it, and charge (program) it in the same way. Picture golden healing light pouring into it through your palm chakras. Breathe through and into your palms, visualizing healing light flowing in from your Crown. Do this for about 10-12 breaths, then place your right hand underneath your left. Create a "cup" with the crystal still on top.

Now, bring your hands and the crystal up to the level of the corresponding chakra, breathing into your hands. Visualize the related color light energy emanating from your hands into the crystal as you breathe, simultaneously feeling sensations within your body. Feeling is the key word; in this day and age, we tend to overthink, and rationalize too much. Feelings, emotions, and instincts are usually missing.

With each breath, draw in this powerful and beautiful healing light energy, seeing the swirling light and life force and feeling it simultaneously. Be open to deep sensations, as this creates a more mystical and spiritually-enhancing experience. Once you are in a synergistic flow and feel completely connected to the crystal and the chakra you are healing, project some *intentions*. The key is to set your intention, project it, and then release it; the process of surrendering - letting go - allows your chakra to fill up with the healing vibrations of the crystal. Once in flow, you should begin to receive some visuals, or visions, from the crystal's consciousness...

This crystal meditation is all about *vision*. The healing properties of the gemstone spark the innate qualities and frequencies of the chakra, so not only will you feel your chakra(s) being unblocked and healed, but you'll also receive flashes of insight or inspiration, or subtle wisdom and messages from the subconscious coupled with your Higher Self. You may have actual visions!

Seven Crystal Chakra Meditation

The second part to this meditation, or another meditation you can perform separately, once you become more experienced with crystals and meditation, is called the "Seven Crystal Chakra Meditation." This one is performed lying down, so it's advised that you get into a comfortable space, complete with all sacred healing items and tools; smudging or sage, incense, music, ambient or minimal lighting, and privacy. Make sure you won't be disturbed, create a comfortable space where you feel safe and held (by Spirit, your angels, whomever you put your trust and faith in).

Place the crystals on your chakras. The Root is located just above your pelvic region, the Sacral is in the center of your stomach, the Solar Plexus is above your abdomen, the Heart is in the center of your chest just across from where your physical heart is, the Throat is directly in the center of your throat, the Third Eye is in the middle of your brow, and the Crown is just above your head, 2-3 inches away.

Once you have found a steady flow of breath and feel content and calm inside, start to ask your crystals for guidance. Ask for:-

- Wisdom
- Guidance
- Subconscious messages
- Divine inspiration
- Repressed emotions to come to light
- Higher Self revelations
- Angelic assistance
- Spirit Animal communication
- Peace and serenity
- Nobility, strength, and integrity
- Higher or universal truths
- Soul growth
- Self-awareness
- Ancient memory
- Past life awareness
- Creative gifts
- Psychic power
- Self-healing abilities
- *Anything you desire!* (Linked to the qualities of any chakra or specific crystal.)

In a lying-down state, your frequency is elevated. You feel more relaxed and at peace, so messages from spirit, the ether, and the astral and subconscious planes can work their magic. Meditation fills you up with empty space, space for creation. Within every atom, there is 99.9% space (scientific fact), the universe - our physical reality - is essentially formless. Meditating with crystals "charges" you with the healing powers and qualities of the crystal, as well as the intentions you set and project. Don't be afraid to ask for what you want; don't live in fear of embracing your power or evolving past the 3D illusions and toxic ways of your younger self. *Crystals want you to elevate and rise...*

Crystal Grid Meditation

Expanding on all the information above, a crystal grid meditation is a bit more advanced. This one requires deep healing music, such as OM chanting, sound mantras, Tibetan singing bowls, a powerful nature music track, or binaural beats. All of the wisdom and techniques in the lying-down meditation applies, however, additionally, you need to set up a crystal grid. You will need **seven crystals relating to the seven main chakras** and **four Quartz crystals**.

Follow the instructions for the previous lying-down meditation, but also place the four Quartz crystals around you; one above your head, one below your feet, and the remaining two either side of you, either at the line of your hips (Root), stomach (Sacral) or chest (Heart).

There is no set-in-stone layout, and you can use your intuition and trust your instincts or dowse with a pendulum to decide the best structure. The Quartz above your head should be just above your Crown, the location known as the *Soul Star chakra*. Oh yes, you have more energy portals! Your Soul Star chakra is incredibly powerful; it connects you to the celestial and heavenly realms and worlds, in addition to the ether, super-consciousness, and higher soul planes. Below your feet, you find your *Earth Star chakra*, the chakra that connects you to sacredness, the grounding energies of Mother Earth, and your ancestors. Both are very powerful, hence why this meditation is known as an *Advanced Crystal Meditation*.

For this meditation, you should perform a 1-3 day fruit fast or water cleanse. You need to detox, so make sure you have some knowledge of fasting and healthy detoxification rituals.

This meditation is particularly powerful for releasing trapped energy in the body. For instance, blocked emotions, repressed wounds, suppressed trauma, painful memories, and family, ancestral, and personal karma. It awakens your kundalini, your primal, psychic, creative, intuitive, and spiritual life force, and further helps with blocks to abundance, love, and longevity. This crystal grid meditation is a miracle-worker due to its power and effect. It has effects on the emotional, psychological, physical, and spiritual planes. It alleviates blocks, coupled with easing dis-ease on a grounded level, while connecting you to a higher consciousness. It provides protection against psychic attack, electromagnetic harm, and negative energies from others and the environment, with potent force. It shields, centers, grounds, energizes, protects, harmonizes, and balances you at highly evolved levels. This meditation is deeply transformative, with potential to lead to powerful revelations, multidimensional insights, and purification that serves as a catalyst to amazing life changes.

This meditation requires you to be in your utmost vibration to truly harness the healing powers of the crystals. A crystal grid meditation is no joke, so make sure you take the wisdom offered seriously. A pure mind, body, and spirit

connection is required; moreover, your mind needs to be open and clear to prevent illusory fears from seeping in.

Once lying down and ready, begin by speaking or thinking the following mantra:

"I am open to receiving the healing energy available... My mind is open, my spirit is cleansed, and my body is relaxed and calm... I am free from fear, with intentions for love and my highest potential strongly in my being. I am receptive to divine inspiration, Merkabah activation, and the awakening of my light body..."

An alternative way to perform this is to hold two of the Quartz crystals in your hands (one in each) with one by your Soul Star and the final one by your Earth Star chakra.

Crystal Treatments (Non-Professional Setting Only)

Once you've become familiar with crystal healing and its ins and outs, you can start experimenting with giving crystal treatments. This can't be offered professionally, of course, as this book doesn't qualify you as a crystal therapist. But you can start utilizing crystal healing powers for self-healing and the good of others. Crystal treatments are a great way to harness the healing energies of crystals while developing a deeper connection with them yourself. Similar to Reiki, an ancient healing art that is becoming increasingly popular in the West, giving a crystal treatment involves scanning the person's aura, hovering your hands over your friend or family member's body, and "tuning in" to their energy. Before attempting crystal treatments, it's essential that you become familiar with the basics of energy work as outlined in the Crystal Meditations. You will need to have spent sufficient time, say, at least a few months, working on yourself; performing self-therapy, making chi balls, practicing the meditations, etc. Then, you can begin a journey of harnessing the healing power of crystals for others.

The crystals are placed around the body, set up specifically to harness their complex electro-magnetic force fields. This energy acts to repolarize any fields that are
misaligned, imbalanced, or in a state of disharmony. This, in turn, restores harmony and balance to both the physical and subtle bodies. Physical hands are never laid directly on the body, or the healer (yourself as the channel) is at risk of picking up the negative energy from the patient. Only experienced energy workers do this. Your hands
should be used to "smooth out" any build-up of trapped energy in the etheric field, which radiates from the physical body up to about 4-6 inches. The crystals correct this imbalanced energy, while your hands concentrate and *direct the flow*.

Preparing To Give a Crystal Treatment

Below, I describe a series of treatments that should be done one after the other on the same day. In essence, they are stages in a single treatment; ideally, all treatments should begin with opening and balancing the chakras. Don't forget that the session should end by *closing* the chakras again, otherwise the client will be too open to outside negative influences. The chakras should only be open when in a safe and loving environment. If you feel comfortable, you can close the chakras with a visualization exercise. One by one, starting at the Crown, visualize the chakra being closed, anticlockwise, like a camera lens iris. To open them, you go the opposite way, envisioning them opening clockwise.

Make sure you have a quiet, warm, and comfortable place for the treatment, and make sure that you will not be disturbed.... Remove any electrical equipment from the room, as these interfere with the magnetic fields, even if they are switched off. Ask your
client or friend to remove any metal objects; watch, jewelry, belts, or coins. Also make sure they are wearing comfortable loose clothing.

Your client (friend or family member only) might like to bathe before a crystal treatment. It is most common to get the client to lie on their back initially, so they can see what you are doing if they wish to do so. You may, however, wish to work on the back during the treatment, in which case they will have to turn face down. Always explain to them what you are doing as they need to take an active part in their healing journey back to wholeness. The ideal direction for working with crystals is the north/south orientation. Their head should point north and their feet south, but this is just a technicality. If you don't have a compass, don't worry too much. If you're in the Southern hemisphere, this orientation should be reversed.

So, you put good energy in (infusing) by moving in a clockwise direction; you take bad energy out (clearing) in an anti-clockwise direction. Rather than "clockwise," it's better to think "sunwise". In other words, when working sunwise, we are in harmony with the natural order of things.

Before beginning any treatment, it's a good idea to cast a *protective circle* around yourself and your client. This is to protect you both from negative energy that may be lingering about. It's very easy; walk around the client clockwise (sunwise) and visualize a cone of white light surrounding you both. It's a bit like an unborn chick, protected inside its shell. You don't need to make a big deal out of it, although it is a ritual - positive (light) spellwork only! Your client may not even know you are doing it, although you can tell them what you are doing to bring them peace of mind. You should then reverse the procedure at the end of the treatment to open the circle before leaving.

To begin, always tune in to the client's Higher Self. Hold your hands above their head, and ask that they be given healing for their highest good. When you complete the treatment, give thanks for what has been received in a similar way. *This is the main intention for providing any crystal treatment or clearing.*

It is important to remember that a treatment will do one or a combination of the following:

1. CLEARING: clearing negative and blocked energy.
2. INSTILLING and BALANCING: replacing the negative energy with positive vibrations while strengthening and building chakra energy, as well as the aura.
3. EXPANDING: for awareness and spiritual development.

Please note that the following information can be performed on yourself too, in any of the Crystal Meditations!

Clearing Technique

1. Starting at the Crown, walk slowly in a clockwise direction, making a circle of energy around the body. This creates an auric seal, a protective bubble of healing light and energy, all in the highest good; with the purest intentions. You will need six crystal points and a generator (a crystal shaped like a wand). Quartz crystal is always great to use.
2. Place a crystal above the Crown pointing upwards. Then, place one crystal on the outside of each knee, forming a triangle with the Crown crystal. Now place one crystal between the feet, pointing upwards, lining it up with the Crown crystal. Place the two remaining crystals at the side of the elbows. This forms a triangle with the crystal at the feet. *You have now created a six-pointed star.*
3. Now, link the energies of the crystals together by holding the generator crystal in both hands with its point facing downwards. Pass the generator seven times over the crystals, then put the generator to one side. Let the client remain in this position for several minutes, basking in the healing light. Remember to speak some intentions, put them at ease with your words, and speak and act without fear. Love is the strongest vibration, and people pick up on it; we're naturally instinctive, empathic, and even telepathic creatures. We pick up on people's thoughts, intentions, and emotions toward us...

Speak and act with love, so your friend or family member will know that they are held in a safe space, as well as being loved and comforted.

4. Next, ask them to slowly become aware of the room and then open their eyes. When they are ready, ask them for any reactions. Did they feel any difference in the new energy? Did they receive any visions or profound images? Did they hear messages from an ancestor, spirit guide, or passed-over loved one? Allow them space to receive the potent energies flowing to them.

5. Finally, you can connect over verbal rapport, bringing them down-to-earth with some knowledge, wisdom, or compassionate words. If the treatment wasn't that high vibration and more grounded, you can try to expand their mind with some esoteric knowledge. Crystal treatments are both down-to-earth - rooted and grounded - and celestial - connected to a higher consciousness.

Step 3 can be repeated as many times as you wish, depending on how long you and your friend wish the session to be. You can also combine *chakra balancing* by placing seven crystals relating to the seven main chakras on top of your friend/family member. Chakra balancing in alignment with a crystal treatment session strengthens the auric field, expands their intuitive and spiritual abilities, and helps to center, ground, and harmonize them.

Opening and Balancing the Chakras

Again, this can be used in harmony with giving a crystal treatment to others or on yourself.

You will need six crystals, as in the clearing technique; 1 crown, 1 feet, 2 knees, and 2 elbows. All should be pointing upwards. First, place seven small crystals over each chakra. all with their points up. Link the outside crystals with your generator, seven times, to form a protective seal. Run the generator straight up from the feet through the chakras to the head, then down from the head to the feet. Do this seven times. You can now balance the chakra energy using the palms of your hands, smoothing out any build-up of energy that you feel or sense. Balance two chakras at a time. Try and feel the build-up of energies with your palms; you can push the energy up and down until a balance is reached.

The best balance combinations are:

CROWN and THROAT
THIRD EYE and HEART
THROAT and SOLAR-PLEXUS
HEART and SACRAL
HEART and ROOT
SACRAL and THIRD EYE
SOLAR-PLEXUS and ROOT

You can focus more energy with your hands or you may wish to instill or draw out energy from any chakra that you feel is under or over-energized. Use the crystal point method described earlier (instilling = point facing down... withdrawing = point facing upwards). Now you can *clear* individual chakras with the clockwise/anticlockwise techniques. Run your sensing hand over the etheric field of the client, feeling into where there may be blocked areas or trapped and repressed energy. This technique is great for emotional, physical, mental, and spiritual wellbeing and balance. It's amazing for restoring harmony, inner equilibrium, and balance to all subtle bodies, as well as sparking new gifts and abilities!

Creative Ideas for Your Healing Techniques:

GROUNDING (earth)

- Root: **Garnet**
- Sacral: **Carnelian**
- Solar Plexus: **Chrysoprase**
- Heart: **Jade**

- Throat: Blue Lace Agate
- Third Eye: Sodalite
- Crown: Blue Kyanite

NEW BEGINNINGS (earth)

- Root: Bloodstone
- Sacral: Rhodonite
- Solar Plexus: Green Tourmaline/Chalcedony
- Heart: Rhodochrosite
- Throat: Celestite
- Third Eye: Blue Sapphire/Turquoise
- Crown: Clear quartz

EMOTIONAL BALANCE (water)

- Root: Smoky Quartz
- Sacral: Aventurine
- Solar Plexus: Green Tourmaline
- Heart: Rose quartz
- Throat: Aquamarine
- Third Eye: Blue Sapphire/Moonstone
- Crown: Clear quartz

RELEASING THE PAST (water)

- Root: Black Tourmalated Quartz
- Sacral: Watermelon Tourmaline
- Solar Plexus: Green tourmaline
- Heart: Pink Tourmaline
- Throat: Aquamarine
- Third Eye: Moonstone
- Crown: Clear quartz

MANIFESTING WISDOM (air)

- Root: Tiger's Eye
- Sacral: Orange Carnelian
- Solar Plexus: Blue Tourmaline/Jade
- Heart: Peridot
- Throat: Aquamarine
- Third Eye: Yellow Topaz/Citrine
- Crown: Diamond/Clear quartz

MAKING CHANGES (fire)

- Root: Tiger's Eye
- Sacral: Orange Carnelian/Amber
- Solar Plexus: Amber/Citrine
- Heart: Ruby/Peridot
- Throat: Aquamarine/Blue lace agate
- Third Eye: Opal/Lapis Lazuli
- Crown: Amethyst/Clear Quartz

Expanding Consciousness

Here is a final layout that can be performed for expanding consciousness and raising your vibration. It's excellent for enhancing spiritual life force, qualities of the Higher Self, and inner power and nobility. You will need: 9 crystals and 1 double terminator.

1. Place the double terminator above the crown.
2. Place a crystal between the feet.
3. Place a crystal on the outside of each foot, pointing outwards.
4. Place a crystal at each ankle, also pointing outwards.
5. Place a crystal on each side of the neck and one at the ears.

All crystals should point outwards. With a generator pointing downwards, link the crystal around the head, starting at the left side of the neck. Move in a clockwise direction, forming a FIGURE OF EIGHT crossing the body at the Root chakra, and forming a circle linking the crystals around the feet. Continue to make a figure of eight seven more times. Stay in this position for around 15 minutes, remembering your breathing, intentions, and balanced state of yin-yang (receptivity/surrender and action/force). If you're performing this on a friend or family member, speak to them gently and with intentions for their healing benefit; describe what you're doing, while giving them instructions.

This is an extremely powerful healing arrangement and should not be used on anyone who has not had several clearing and energizing treatments, or at the very least has been working with crystals for a long period of time.

4

Crystals for the Star Signs

In my other book about 'Astrology and Crystals', a brief list for each star sign is mentioned. In this book, we explore the "crystal personalities" of each of the 12 star signs. In other words, which crystals are best for each zodiac sign and the *personality blueprint* of each sign, as embodied in the crystal!

Aries

Passionate Garnet

I am Garnet, a passionate and vital stone, representing powerful life force, enthusiasm, and inspired action. I take action with will, confidence, and excitement - I am not at all weak or shy. I live my life unapologetically, free from fear, and with total self-respect. Self-preservation, a need for stability, and unbreakable desires for intimacy and companionship define me; I have a lot of sexual energy, as well as instincts to shine and conquer. I love coming out on top, being first, and winning. I am the gemstone that brings vital life force, devotion, love, passion, increased sensuality, inspiration, and purification. I can help you shine, be more confident, and find your authentic voice without fear of judgment or psychic attack. I am the perfect crystal for Aries' personality to shine... Moreover, I activate hidden soul talents linked to physical stamina, strength, and fitness. I like to be active, move about, and live my life with an evolved sense of motivation to achieve and conquer. In love and business, I like to win! I am fiercely protective of my security, self-esteem, and loved ones, so I can teach you how to be as independent as a tiger or tigress, without the aggression or intimation.

Loving Carnelian

I am Carnelian, a stone of emotional warmth, sociability, individuality, happiness, and courage. I bring positivity, creative inspiration, rebirth, transformation, and harmony. I increase your capacity for past life recall, as well as friendliness and self-esteem in personal relationships. As one of Aries' stones, I represent inner fire, optimism, confidence, authentic communication, and a direct and assertive tone. I can help you find your voice, speak and act without fear, and act on your sensual, creative, and sexual needs. Emotions soar with me, I amplify emotional wisdom, intelligence, and sensitivity. Like Aries, I am bold, passionate, and expressive, yet I also have a sensitive side. To unravel the depths of my soulful nature, you must be willing to be more vulnerable, without compromising your independent, courageous, and dominant side. Connect with me when you need to tame your inner rage, envy, and burning jealousies or negativities... I am perfect for bringing out Aries' greatest strengths.

Competitive Diamond

Like me, the Diamond, one of the rarest gemstones to be found on planet Earth, Aries is unique. I am hard and strong, tough with incredible stamina and endurance. I grow through immense pressure, and this symbolizes the Aries spirit. Like me, they are warriors, fearless, always up for a heated debate or fight - to win and succeed - and desire nothing more than to be seen as the best. I am the *most* hardy crystal on planet Earth! In addition to my strength and sheer determination to come out on top, I represent purity, harmony, love, abundance, and prosperity. I develop feelings of companionship, intimacy, and commitment - I am ideal for soulmate bonds and romantic love. I also bring optimism, confidence, self-esteem, inner clarity, and wholeness; I can balance your subtle bodies. Aries can learn to be more pure in thought and speech with my help, due to being ruled by Mars, the planet of competition, war, and aggression. I increase endurance, nobility, inner strength, a sense of invincibility, and devotion is a method that combats egocentricity simultaneously. Serenity, shining in the spotlight, graciousness, sensitivity, and soul talents and aspirations come out with me.

Taurus

Emotionally Intelligent Emerald

I am Emerald, an ideal stone for Taurus' romantic, loving, and intuitive nature. I increase clairvoyance, faith, trust, harmony, wholeness, and inner stability, as well as duties, practicalities, and responsibilities... with an empathic touch! I enhance compassion, feelings of friendship, intimacy, and romance, and intuition at high levels. I nurture instincts to make positive change, as well as joy, happiness, and serenity. I am calming and balancing with a sense of devotion. Also, practical awareness coupled with clear vision and commitment to a higher truth, universal truths, and devotional love increase with me. My energy, like Taurus, is nurturing, benevolent, and wise. I bring love, positive feelings of warmth and connection, and emotional intelligence, while stimulating subtle strength, courage, and optimistic growth. I can assist you in finding deeper joy, insight, wisdom, positivity, and hope that the world is fair, just, and kind. Consciousness expands, so call on me if you need to help taming the inner Bull.

Wise Malachite

I am Malachite, wise, self-leading, balanced, understanding, and loyal. Similar to Taurus' energy, I am comforting, a real friend in need, and a gem to loved ones. I enhance inner serenity, protection, ancient wisdom, self-knowledge, and healing. I can aid in positive transformation, as well as your ability to access spiritual guidance. I am a stone to turn to for deep cleansing, transformation, and protection from electromagnetic harm, environmental pollution, and negative energies. I can be connected with for depth, emotional intelligence, alchemical powers linked to empathy, kindness, and compassion, and nurturing. I nurture yet expand, soothe yet energize, and heal and empower simultaneously. I connect you with an ancient wisdom and unique type of self-alignment that allows you to transmute, empower yourself, alchemize negativity into positivity and ignorance to knowledge, and heal on the deepest levels. I can clear and activate your chakras, spark creative and spiritual inspiration, and alleviate pain, trauma, and heartache. I am ideal for Taurus' sweet and caring personality.

Compassionate Rose Quartz

Like Taurus, I am a symbol for self-love, romance, caring, kindness, friendship, and selflessness. I am linked to Venus, just as Taurus is ruled by Venus. I enhance platonic intimacy, motherly love, sensuality, empathy, and compassion, as well as tolerance, patience, understanding, emotional sensitivity, and generosity. I amplify devotional qualities, including universal love, unconditional love, self-respect, nobility, integrity, grace, morality, and purity of mind, thought, and action. I help to harmonize the mind, body and spirit connection without compromising on grounding or material awareness. I am both spiritually and physically enhancing, as well as balancing the psychological and emotional bodies. I am Rose Quartz, the stone of love! Taurus' best gentle and empathic qualities can be strengthened with integrity, while forgiveness, acceptance, and the ability to heal from pain and trauma release. Clearing wounds of the past are essential for you to step into greatness, self-leadership, and emotional and psychological intelligence.

Gemini

Communicative Chrysocolla

I am communicative Chrysocolla, ideal for Gemini's expressive and upbeat personality. Tranquility, serenity, peace, subconscious wisdom, intuition, patience, and tolerance increase, in addition to my energy enhancing acceptance, gentleness, sensitivity, honesty, intuition, and higher truth. I am committed to unraveling life's deeper meanings, mysteries, and truths, and devote my life to sharpening my mental abilities. Like Gemini, I am a master communicator with powerful wit, intellect, and mental agility. I can alternate between various topics, conversations, and themes of discussion. I love a debate, yet can keep my cool, combined with charm and charisma. Calmness, peace, clarity, insight, vision, authenticity, and logic define me; I am a master of analysis, perception, and observation... I can help Gemini to strengthen their natural gifts while bringing some sensitivity, emotional maturity, and gentleness into the mix. I alleviate guilt and pain so you can shine in a social setting without shame or suppression. I instill confidence, self-awareness, psychic vision, potent instincts, and creativity.

Truthful Topaz

I am Topaz, truthful, honest, and incredibly wise. I amplify communicative powers, fortune, luck, good health, wealth, and attraction. I amplify, enhance, and energize Gemini's good qualities. I soothe, stimulate, recharge, and increase joy, generosity, and abundance, while helping you to access imaginative, cerebral, and logical gifts. I am deeply intelligent, yet just as kind and sincere. Motivational qualities expand with my help, so I am perfect for bringing out Gemini's best qualities; analytical power, logic, higher reasoning, intuition, integrity, and transparency. I can help you master storytelling! Also, smoothing out any tendencies to distort truth, gossip, or get up to mischief with such a powerful intellect and mind. I recharge, cleanse, and balance your chakras and subtle energy bodies, and promote truth, forgiveness, and confidence in expressing yourself. Gifts, wisdom, and courage to express your emotions shine with me. I am the stone for Gemini's higher self, because I encourage transparent and direct communication; assertiveness, willpower, and nobility are given a chance to shine... Further, with my help, you can overcome stress, tension, and anxiety to feel more centered and at peace.

Assertive Tiger's Eye

I, like Gemini, am assertive, empowered, and self-authoritative. I enhance integrity, willpower, courage, grounding, protection, and grace. I increase your desire to express yourself, stand strong in your truth, and speak with clarity and conviction - I encourage authenticity, as well as integrity, truth, and self-knowledge. Through expanding wisdom, you find your confidence and courage, which in turn increases problem-solving, smooth social interactions, and a sense of fun. I amplify joy, positivity, social charm, warmth, sophistication, class, and ambition. I am here to bring out your dominant traits, so you can shine, teach, lead, inspire, and educate others through your wisdom. I know you are self-aware, deeply bright and enthusiastic about life and all it has to offer too. So, connect with me when you want some inspiration, motivation, or masculine assertiveness and strength. I mix business with pleasure, responsibility with joy, and practicalities with fun! I am the perfect stone for cerebral and upbeat Gemini. Clear thinking, ancient wisdom, focus, motivation, balanced yin and yang energy, purpose, and mental clarity expand with me, in addition to powerful luck and protection.

Cancer

Empathic Moonstone

I am Moonstone, a gemstone ideal for Cancer, due to my mothering, selfless, and instinctive energy. I represent good fortune, hope, spiritual insight, new beginnings, ancient wisdom, sacred and self-knowledge, and profound intuition. I amplify emotional intelligence, empathy, and sensitivity, qualities unique to Cancer. I amplify abundance, esoteric knowledge, inner knowing, psychic powers, and spiritual abilities, bringing the best out of sweet and sensitive Cancer. I amplify feminine energy, insight, foresight, stability, inner strength, and compassion, as well as the energy of new beginnings. I help with childbirth, pregnancy, and menstrual and reproductive cycles, something unique to the Cancer sign. (For men, I can help you support your lover better!) Selflessness, imagination, depth, vulnerability, authenticity, inspiration, and self-love increase through my energy. Overall, my frequency is perfect for Cancer because we're the ideal match; Cancer embodies my energy to perfection, so working with me will sharpen, strengthen, and fine-tune what's innate within you.

Generous Ruby

I amplify good fortune, nurturing, selflessness, spiritual sight, and hope, as well as happiness, abundance, and ancient wisdom. I am a stone for the heart, thus increasing empathic, caring, and compassionate qualities. I can show you how to love yourself, care for yourself, and shine with tolerance, patience, and understanding. I am ideal for all matters of family, friendship, and intimate relationships, both romantic and business. I inspire growth, inner strength, security, and stability, as well as new beginnings and companionship. I can enhance luck and love while ingraining new philosophies and beliefs systems that can help with your soul's journey to enlightenment. Ideal for Cancer's spiritual and deeply sensitive nature, I nurture sensitivities in a way that equally allows for strong boundaries. Emotions can be stabilized and balanced with my assistance, and as a stone of romantic and selfless love, I empower sensitive and spiritually advanced Cancer to come out of their shell. Strength and humility entwine in an energetic dance that enables shy, reserved, and submissive Cancer to rise from the depths of the sea... like a mermaid rediscovering their soul spark.

Spiritual Selenite

One of Cancer's faithful companions, I am a stone for meditation, universal consciousness, clarity of thought, subtle perception, and purification. I help you embody greater peace, purity, psychic instincts, subtle and spiritual powers to shine and find your voice, and higher perspectives. I enhance clarity and logic, so you can tap into intellectual and analytical gifts - something you often neglect. I enhance optimism and positive thinking, while connecting you with the higher realms of angelic contact, celestial insights, and divine wisdom. I support sensitive, empathic, compassionate, generous, and selfless personalities, also energizing integrity, nobility, and diplomacy. Cancer's compassion combined with unconditional love is unmatched, yet my faith, spiritual essence, and intuition are matched; I am ideal for the nurturing Crab. I can enhance awareness of past lives too, as well as seeing the bigger picture, living with depth, and finding your sense of purpose and innocence.

Leo

Confident Sunstone

I am Sunstone, a crystal of freedom, originality, luck, intelligence, and innovation. I represent extreme independence, as well as sensuality, self-expression, and courage. I am confident, bold, fortune and abundance-bringing, and empowered. I enhance joy, logic, intellect, wit, intuition, imagination, resourcefulness, ambition, and self-esteem, in addition to optimism and warmth. I spark your inner glow, so you can live your life unapologetically, like a lion or lioness, but with grace, tact, and sensitivity. I am a sophisticated gemstone, amplifying innate dominant, assertive, and communicative qualities unique to Leo natives. Leo is ruled by the Sun; therefore, there is no stone more suited to perfect and fine-tune your strengths... I can increase intuition, alleviate stress, ease social anxiety, calm nerves combined with an overactive mind, and set up clear boundaries. I promote enthusiasm, self-empowerment, and self-healing mechanisms of the body; I am excellent for overcoming codependency, attention-seeking tendencies, and a lack of emotional intelligence.

Romantic Rhodonite

I am romantic and elegant Rhodonite, a stone of delicacy, diplomacy, and sensitivity. I amplify romantic needs and feelings while instilling deep peace and clarity for intimate interactions. All relationships get a boost with me because I combine emotional sensitivity and vulnerability with inner strength and stamina. I am strong-willed, but I am also romantic, soft, and courteous. I can align you with your inner path, purpose, destiny, soul's mission, or core strengths and talents. I can help you find your truth and inner voice, and then speak it. As Leo is known for being egotistical, arrogant, and loud - always wanting to be the center of attention - I can help you tone down your inner fire without compromising on your needs or desires. I amplify healthy self-esteem in a way that allows you to shine, have wonderful intimate relationships, and not bulldoze over anyone. I am peaceful, serene, and emotionally balanced. I clear emotional wounds, scars, and traumas so past pain can be released. I am Rhodonite, I ground and harmonize yin and yang energies, powerful for emotional and intellectual and feminine and masculine unification. Abuse, lack of forgiveness, shock, pain, confusion, self-destruction, and narcissism can be healed and overcome.

Powerful Pyrite

I am powerful Pyrite, symbolizing logic, creativity, optimism, learning, perception, and intelligence. I promote mental stability, higher intelligence, memory, clarity, and psychic development, also energizing self-protective abilities. I can shield you from harmful and negative energy, so you remember how powerful and intelligent you are. There's no need to let others dull your sparkle, Leo; you are a fiery, passionate, and optimistic individual who faces challenges head-on. You're assertive and strong-willed, a natural boss too. I help to remind you of your greatness while simultaneously encouraging meditation, serenity, and devotion to your Higher Self and life purpose. Electromagnetic harm - vibrations from the ether and environment that may interfere with your spirit and intellect - are combated with my protective energy. I balance the subtle energy bodies, spark potent instincts to protect, serve, and nurture, and help to merge intuition and psychic gifts with rationality and wit. Mental abilities come to life with me, yet I also offer assistance for divination and both emotional and spiritual growth. I am here to remind you that you can be intellectual and live with faith and trust in the divine.

Virgo

Intellectual Peridot

I am Peridot, a stone for healing, purification, rebirth, growth, comfort, and intuition. I amplify intellectual and relaxation gifts while bringing renewal, transformation, and awakening on the intellectual, emotional, and spiritual planes. I cleanse, align, ground, balance, and purify. I release and neutralize negative toxins and impurities that may negatively affect your ability to think, analyze, and perceive clearly; this is also known as "psychic debris." I bring warmth, stability, peace, serenity, clarity, and calmness to multiple planes, while inspiring educational and professional pursuits. I can help you ground and center without becoming lost in work - I assist in overcoming workaholic tendencies. I can help with jealousy, spite, resentment, irritation, bitterness, greed, and anger. I expand joy, self-care, self-love, optimistic thinking, expansion, and a deeper desire to travel and explore, qualities which are ideal for Virgo's small-minded nature. Perfectionism, only paying attention to the smaller details, and cynicism can be overcome. I reduce stress, open your heart to new relationships, heal apathy, and encourage responsibility and confidence; my energy amplifies self-worth, self-esteem, and personal empowerment in a way that compliments Virgo's subtle nature.

Nurturing Jasper

I am relaxing and nurturing Jasper, bringing contentment, tranquility, healing, completion, and compassion. I inspire healing, personal growth, and deep insight that combines spiritual perspectives with rational and analytical thought. Virgo is known for being small-minded - closed off to bigger-picture philosophies and spiritual themes; I help Virgo come out of their intellectual bubble... Without neglecting core psychological strengths. I am known as the Supreme Nurturer, so I balance and merge emotional intelligence and sensitivity with mental gifts. I can sustain and support you through times of stress, difficulty, and hardship, any life challenge that involves tension and struggle. I bring wholeness, harmony, and inner serenity, in addition to wit, quick-thinking, imagination, and assertiveness. I enhance grace, diplomacy, and compromise, as well as balancing yin (feminine) and yang (masculine) energies. This is great for Virgo because you are a yin earth sign with a yang ruler, Mercury. I can protect and shield you from electromagnetic harm, while motivating you to transform ideas into action...

Stable Green Aventurine

I am Green Aventurine, a stone of independence, prosperity, and success, as well as security, stability, and inner strength. I represent empathy, tolerance, compassion, self-love, gentleness, and sensitivity, as well as intelligence, wit, and logic. I am ideal for emotional and psychological balance. Abundance, emotional intelligence, powerful intellect, intuition, and innovation amplify with my energy. I enhance sociability, patience, understanding and higher sight, without compromising Virgo's key qualities, which are rooted in material and practical respect, grounding and responsibility. I amplify avenues to securing security, as well as leadership, self-autonomy, self-worth, and self-control to overcome anger, frustrations, and people-pleasing. I can help you let go of codependency, clouded judgment, intolerance, a know-it-all pedantic attitude, and intellectual superiority. I restore balance and sensitivity, so you can be more of a team-player and compromising individual.

Perseverance, determination, tenacity, subtle ambition, instincts, intuition, and amazing organizational skills all amplify with me.

Libra

Wise Lapis Lazuli

I am Lapis Lazuli, a symbol for inner power, purification, intuition, manifestation, and friendship. I enhance truth, universal consciousness, spirituality, meditation, and positive alchemy, as well as light magic, confidence, self-esteem, powerful expression, and communication. I instill deep insight, subconscious wisdom, universal love, protection from psychic attack and negative energy, and access to dreams. I am ideal for naturally intellectual and spiritually gifted Libra, because I can help you connect to the dream, astral, and multidimensional planes. Honesty, integrity, nobility, morality, and majesty expand. I can activate your higher mind and Third Eye in a way that allows your best abilities to come through. I amplify peace, clarity, perception, intellectualism, imagination, spiritual illumination, and protection from psychic attack. I stand for truth, self-love, and forgiveness, qualities that can help with Libra's codependent and people-pleasing side. I can inspire you to share your knowledge, talents, and wisdom to help others, as well as accessing advanced creative and artistic gifts. Further, all cerebral and higher-minded gifts shine through with my assistance...

Balanced Jade

I am balanced Jade, a stone of fertility, serenity, and wisdom, as well as practicality, harmony, peace, tranquility, stability, and wisdom. I help Libra fine-tune what's innate within you. I am ideal for your nurturing and feminine, and ambitious and assertive sides. I help you find moderation, self-autonomy, and independence while not sacrificing your caring, loyal, sensitive, nurturing, and intuitive side. Venus makes you deep, spiritually evolved, and emotionally intelligent, in addition to romantic, sensitive, submissive, and lovers of beauty and pleasure. As a balanced stone, I am here to bring the qualities of Venus and masculine air traits out in you! I spark protection, self-love, dreams, sacred knowledge, wisdom of divine and universal law and order, and kinship. As a crystal of tranquility, practicality, and fertility, I amplify longevity, inner peace, and the ability to both form and keep long-term friendships. I can help with romantic, business, and family partnerships.

Imaginative Opal

I am imaginative Opal, an alluring stone to enhance loyalty, love, peace, independence, and faithfulness. As Libra can be quite flirtatious and self-sovereign, I am excellent for grounding playful energies into something long-lasting, which can help with intimate relationships. I inspire commitment, creativity within relationships, and imagination. I love to help you find your freedom without losing touch of the practicalities of life. Intellect, logic, intuition, imagination, and creative originality and innovation expand with me. I bring emotional stability, balance, and serenity, as well as mood balancing and stabilizing. I enhance cosmic consciousness, higher mental gifts, self-sovereignty, healthy attachments, vision, and psychic awareness. I am ideal for finding balance between self-autonomy - your freedom, and social bonds and connections. I elevate your capacity for mystical visions, which can help with art, music, and professional ventures. I am Opal, a beautiful stone for Venus-ruled Libra's empathic personality.

Scorpio

Transformative Turquoise

I am transformative Turquoise, a stone of purification, protection, and wisdom, as well as balance, strength, positivity, optimistic thinking, and self-knowledge. I enhance communication, resourcefulness, and ambition coupled with empathy, tolerance, and compassion. I work on the emotional and psychological planes while balancing the spiritual and physical bodies, and further restoring harmony to internal distortions and imbalances. I am excellent for reconnecting to your source of personal power, self-authoritative, and alchemical abilities. I promote friendship, love, intimacy, self-pleasure, and partnerships, instilling strength, grace, and tact. Mindful and empathic communication soars with me. My energy transmutes, inspires, and uplifts, as well as connecting you to ancient wisdom that opens imaginative, intellectual, and spiritual doorways. Intuition, emotional intelligence, sensitivity, romance, and intellect increase and expand. I help to protect you from harmful energy, in addition to stabilizing your mood and alleviating depression or isolating tendencies.

Ambitious Citrine

I am ambitious Citrine, a stone of creativity, pleasure, prosperity, happiness, and abundance. I represent pleasure, confidence, comfort, success, and truth, as well as alignment, moderation, and balance. I can help you to be more generous and compassionate while finding powerful ambition, luck, and manifestation abilities simultaneously. I am here to help you find great joy! This is something Scorpio's depressive and melancholic nature often needs help with. As a crystal for spiritual growth, warmth, and goodness, I enhance nobility, grace, and social charm and charisma. Creative visions, intellect, and imagination all shine with me. I align your chakras, balance your subtle energy bodies, and amplify psychic gifts, in harmony with deep desires to make money, achieve wealth, and find professional accomplishments in life. Achievement is my aim. I can assist in assimilating life experiences, finding deeper wonder and joy, embodying self-esteem and self-worth, and strengthening mental clarity, focus, and concentration. I help to alleviate fears, traumas, and depression, in addition to balancing the emotions. My energy is energizing, recharging, and soothing on multiple planes... Like Scorpio, I am a master manifester, who combines desires for prosperity with spiritual gifts and sight.

Emotionally Intelligent Malachite

I am Malachite, a gemstone of loyalty, leadership, and ancient wisdom. I am powerfully comforting, balancing, and transformative, also being a symbol for healing, profound self-knowledge, wisdom of past lives, spirituality, and meditation. I increase divination, self-healing, and transcendental awareness - deep states of peace, contentment, and self-alignment. I expand protection, self-understanding, higher spiritual guidance, unconditional love, universal compassion, empathy, tolerance, patience, and faithfulness. I can enhance your intimate and business relationships while helping you find deeper meaning, intimacy, and self-love in your life. I alchemize and transmute negative energy, as well as helping you transcend toxic cycles, codependency, karmic patterns, bad habits, and self-sabotaging behaviors. As a sign associated with shamanism and shadow work and integration, I am ideal for depth, intensity, and all matters of shadow and spiritual healing. I stimulate dreams, spark ancient and subconscious wisdom, and help you come to terms with old pains, heartache, and wounds of the soul. Your spirit body comes alive, while physical, emotional, and psychological imbalances are soothed and healed. Seeing through illusions and uncovering BS or hidden motives can also be achieved.

Sagittarius

Truth-Seeking Labradorite

I am Labradorite, a stone of higher truth, vision, and intuition. I am here to show you how to be more honest, sincere, and direct in your dealings. I aid in communication, assertive expression, and mindfulness, combining these masculine gifts with sensitivity and spiritual awareness. You can integrate emotional intelligence and vulnerability with powerful psychological and intuitive gifts, which is where you thrive. I am a symbol for higher consciousness, personal and universal truth, nobility, selflessness, and service. I help you access hidden psychic and spiritual gifts while energizing and strengthening perceptive, intuitive, and imaginative powers. I am the stone for honesty and transparency at high and noble levels, in a way that can push you to become a teacher or elder in your profession, service, or trade. I connect you with ancient wisdom, potent analytical and logical abilities, and fine-tuned perception that increases multidimensional awareness. I strengthen willpower, originality, and clairvoyance, as well as aligning you with your Higher Self in daily, waking life affairs. Patience, perseverance, ambition, breakthroughs, and seeing through illusions, increase with me. I help with fears, doubts, anxieties, insecurities, and trust in yourself and the universe...

Wise Amethyst

I am wise and majestic Amethyst, an excellent stone for Sagittarius' noble and free spirit. I amplify nobility, peace, calmness, intuition, psychic and spiritual gifts, meditation, and higher self-awareness. I protect you from psychic attack and negative energies, as well as the BS and illusions or manipulations of the world. I help you activate your inner BS detector! Communication, tact, wit, honesty, personal power, self-authority, and higher truths and ideals expand with me. I am ideal for bringing grounding and practical awareness to your impulsive, impatience, and reckless-immature nature. You're known for being frivolous, as well as totally impulsive, which makes you lack maturity and depth; I help to stabilize and center you. I increase passion and joy for the things that set your soul on fire, so this in turn sparks healing. I can help protect you against sadness, anger, and pain, calming your temper and enhancing inner serenity and contentment. Telepathy between friends and lovers increase, cleansing, purification, and clearing expand, and self-worth and self-esteem merge with a desire to spread truth and knowledge, for the benefit of others. I have a sobering effect that can help against indulging, instant gratification, and addictions or drug or alcohol consumption. I dispel negative energy while enhancing optimism, courage, and joy.

Optimistic Carnelian

I am Carnelian, ideal for Sagittarius' fiery, warm, and sociable nature. I enhance individuality, creativity, self-esteem, vitality, friendliness, sensuality, and a love of love, friendship, and sexual intimacy. I expand creative and artistic gifts, in addition to friendships, soulmate connections, and platonic and sexual intimacy - all things Sagittarius the Centaur loves. I thrive in a creative environment, and can help you to be more playful, expressive, and extroverted. But I increase empathy and sensitivity in equal measure, encouraging depth and vulnerability. Life force, imagination, energy, courage, devotion, kinship, romance, libido, innovation, originality, and independence all increase with me. I am an amazing crystal to bring out Sagittarius' best qualities because I represent your personality holistically. Ruled by the Archer, who reaches for the stars, and Centaura, half animal and half man simultaneously, I am ideal for Sagittarius' need for both higher philosophical and creative connections and a passionate lifestyle. I promote happiness, physical instincts, rebirth, transformation, emotional warmth, generosity, and selflessness, in addition to the positive pursuit of pleasure... so pleasure doesn't become destructive. I can help with anger, fear, and rage without compromising passion or excitability.

Capricorn

Headstrong Onyx

I am Onyx, headstrong, self-controlled, persevering, and energetic with immense physical stamina and strength, all the qualities of Capricorn. I increase grounding, practicality, intelligence, instincts, confidence, fortune, prosperity, decisiveness, and responsibility. Also, a sense of duty, purpose, and personal power. I amplify ambition, self-authority, happiness, self-esteem, fortune, determination, steadfastness, and tenacity. Capricorn's true light shines through with my energy because I am an embodiment of this tenacious and modest earth sign. I can help you overcome grief associated with trauma and emotional wounds, especially great for Capricorn because your shadow includes emotional aloofness and detachment. Saturn's energy is amplified with me, which connects you to your source of power, truth, and self-autonomy even deeper. I am as headstrong, tenacious, and steadfast as they come!

Grounded Jet

I am Jet, a crystal representing emotional balance, grounding, and moderation, as well as harmony, wholeness, and integration. I am here to remind you of your goals, align you with your purpose, and discover your strength. I increase methodological and analytical thinking coupled with innovation, problem-solving, and instincts. Powerful intuition and self-protective measures can be found with me. I shield you from negative energy while energizing ambitions, a high-flying mindset, and forgiveness; the ability to forgive, let go, and right your wrongs. I spark emotional, physical, psychological, and spiritual healing. I fine-tune hidden talents and strengths so you can live unapologetically. I am your companion when you need to overcome anxiety, depression, and fears or insecurities, specifically regarding your career or life path, further bringing awareness to emotional traumas, negative patterns of conditioning, and emotional aloofness or avoidance. I help you get clear, be honest, and take accountability of your emotions and feelings! Finally, I am the perfect gemstone for grounding fantasies and visions into tangible form, which can help with daydreaming tendencies or a lack of maturity and life experience. I help with physical pain linked to hard work too. I'm an excellent stone for wealth, prosperity, and protection.

Insightful Sodalite

I am insightful, wise, and discerning Sodalite, complementary to Capricorn's humble and intellectual nature. I symbolize truth, perception, and clarity, as well as logic, higher reasoning, intuition, emotional balance, objectivity, and self-esteem. I can help you think more intuitively and imaginatively when you have been relying on analysis or rationality for too long. Spiritual sight and visions increase with me, yet they're connected to mental gifts and psychological power, which suits you perfectly. I am a stone of wisdom, self-knowledge, contentment, peace of mind, serenity, and reflection. I am here when you need to contemplate, analyze, and introspect. I also bring balance to the physical and spiritual bodies and planes and the emotional and psychological bodies. Tolerance, patience, acceptance, understanding, empathy, and depth expand. I lighten and deepen simultaneously, which means I bring joy and lightness coupled with depth and intensity. As a magnetic feminine earth sign with a dominant masculine ruler, Saturn, this is a wonderful blend of energies. I balance, harmonize, and unify, so you can attain self-realization, enlightenment, and self-evolution.

Aquarius

Visionary Aquamarine

I am visionary and cleansing Aquamarine, ideal for peace, cleansing, meditation, tranquility, and higher analytical and imaginative thinking. I increase inner strength, power, and nobility. I enhance emotional intelligence and empathy, while merging it with cerebral and cognitive gifts. I work on the emotional and psychological planes, ideal for Aquarius the 'Water-Bearer,' who transforms and alchemizes feelings and instincts into higher thought-forms. I am idealistic, prophetic, wise, serene, and compassionate. I symbolize higher power and truth, as well as universal unity, love, and justice. I bring peace, prophetic wisdom, calmness, contentment, and mental clarity. Also, greater sensitivity, nobility, and righteousness - spiritual enlightenment is available with my energy. I promote self-expression and peaceful, empathic, and mindful communication; consciousness expands. I am Aquamarine, a beautiful stone for cerebral Aquarius, with a strong sense of empathy and altruism. I can strengthen your aura, align your chakras, and help you to make sense of tricky emotions, feelings, and inner-world sensations. Furthermore, I enhance tolerance, understanding, and non-judgement at high levels.

Independent Opal

I am independent Opal, a stone of consciousness, faithfulness, loyalty, love, and serenity. I bring independence, self-autonomy, and self-reflection without sacrificing a need for depth, intimacy, or friendship. As you, Aquarius, are known for being aloof and emotionally distant, I can help you to stabilize and harmonize your emotions without feeling too vulnerable. With me, you retain your sovereignty, just becoming softer and more mature and sensitive. Relationships expand. I assist with emotional intelligence, balance, and maturity, in addition to psychic and mystical visions. I increase intuition, instincts, self-awareness, self-knowledge, and knowledge of sacred and universal laws and order. I can connect you to the divine spark within, which has positive effects on a range of planes, from intellect to imagination and physical vibrancy to spiritual gifts. I inspire conscious action in the realm of love, career, and professional and educational connections. I am Opal, perfect for bringing out your strengths! I also amplify self-worth, creativity, originality, memory, spontaneity, and personal power, as well as helping you calm anger and aggression.

Expressive Azurite

I am expressive Azurite, the stone to work with for enlightenment, past life recall, ancient wisdom, divine knowledge, and personal power and authority. I activate hidden memories regarding your soul purpose, also aligning you with a higher and cosmic truth. I simulate psychic, intuitive, spiritual, intellectual, imaginative, and spiritual gifts, as well as higher cerebral, mental, and cognitive gifts. I am excellent for all professional and educational pursuits while increasing passion for cultural and creative activities. I help with fine-tuning artistic gifts! I awaken your inner peacock, so you can shine without fear of judgment or insecurities projected out into the world; confidence, self-esteem, prestige, success, and happiness increase with me. Meditation, channeling, healing, humanitarianism, big-picture thinking, and Higher Self awareness amplify in abundance. I can spark your Crown and Third Eye to initiate new pathways and modes of expression. I nurture communication, justice, courage, diplomacy, kindness, mindfulness, pragmatic action, inspiration, and motivation to overcome laziness or apathy. Fears can be released calmly and with grace and tact; moreover, I increase social charisma, charisma, and speaking skills. Positive thinking expands.

Pisces

Psychic Amethyst

I am Amethyst, the perfect stone for Pisces' psychic, spiritual, and intuitive nature. I represent healing, peace, clairvoyance, spiritual awareness and illumination, nobility, and majesty. I am a crystal of higher truth, subconscious wisdom, dream states, transcendental meditation, and purification. I heal the mind, body, and soul, bring emotional balance, and energize cerebral and psychological gifts. I am excellent for Pisces' submissive and sensitive nature, as I combine strength and nobility with intuition and emotional intelligence. I aid in self-protection, protection from negative energies and psychic attack, and stress and anxiety release, in addition to sobering addictions, imbalances, and internal distortions or faulty belief systems picked up on. With ancient ruler Jupiter, it's easy for Pisces to become somewhat fanatic or self-righteous with regard to your spiritual power, in addition to the "illusion and fantasy" aspect of Neptune. I enhance power, strength, and self-alignment while allowing you to see through illusions. I am a BS detector! I sharpen intuition coupled with innate mystical, healing, and creative gifts tenfold. Positive transformation, cleansing, purification, soul alignment, angelic and divine communication, focus, memory, and spiritual wisdom enhance with me. I can help you be more assertive and direct in your communication without compromising core sensitive and gentle qualities.

Prophetic Aquamarine

I am prophetic Aquamarine, a stone of prosperity, serenity, peace, inspiration, and prophecy. I amplify inner truth, alignment, meditation, tranquility, inner strength, majesty, and nobility. Known as the Stone of Prophets and Healers, I am ideal for Pisces' dreamy, contemplative, and introspective nature. I bring out potent psychic, spiritual, and healing gifts, as well as connecting you to psychic instincts, intuition, and clairvoyance. I enhance non-judgement, tolerance, patience, compassion, universal love, empathy, sensitivity, ancient wisdom, self-knowledge, courage, devotional qualities, discipline, and soul alignment. I can help you find your purpose, true passions, and life path. I align you with your destiny or soul mission, helping you to discover hidden talents and divine manifestations of a higher consciousness. I enhance empathic, healing, and alchemical abilities that can make you into someone self-mastered, or a healer, therapist, psychic, seer, or spiritual teacher. Emotional intelligence, wisdom, and maturity get a boost, while a deeper sense of responsibility and inspiration can be amplified. I amplify clairvoyance, clairsentience, and clairaudience, as well as telepathic and dreaming and astral capabilities. I shield the aura, align and harmonize the chakras, and promote positive self-talk and mindsets. I can help with low moods, depression, apathy, and fears or anxieties that prevent you from leaving the house. Finally, I clear confusions, illusions, and blocks to enlightenment and self-mastery.

Serene Jade

I am serene Jade, excellent for fertility, wisdom, practicality, nurturing, and caring. I increase compassionate and empathic qualities while enhancing new perspectives, fresh ideas, and luck. I enhance Pisces' natural generous, kind, and selfless nature, in addition to amplifying balance, harmony, inner stability, practical awareness, longevity, and sustainable and ethical practices. I can help with the Pisces shadow traits of impracticality, ungrounding, irresponsibility with finances, and a lack of boundaries. I can help Pisces take better care of yourself, attend to personal needs, and live with more self-respect and self-care measures. Sacred knowledge, psychic and visionary gifts, creativity, originality, independence, harmonious relationships, and self-protection expand and amplify. I energize emotional sensitivity and intelligence, as well as the ability to react to chaotic and dangerous or uncool situations with calmness, grace, and saintlike patience. I help you master submissiveness that allows for peace and rationality with a unique type of assertiveness, self-authority, and personal power. Self-sufficiency, self-autonomy, friendship, fortune, luck, and manifestation powers linked to love and money increase. I am Jade, a stone for insightful dreams, astral projection, purity, authentic living, finding your voice, and speaking your truth.

Conclusion

Crystals, chakras, and astrology form a new 'holy trinity!' To find wholeness, harmony, and equilibrium, turn your sights to this new trinity. Like the mind, body, and spirit connection, whereby all three need to retain balance and unity, crystals, chakras, and astrology are three pillars to self-evolution. Soul talents come to life, past karmas and wounds can be released, and new beginnings coupled with unlimited potential are in store. Astrology teaches us to look towards the stars, while crystals show us the powers innate within. Vice versa is also true, and this is why the wisdom contained in this book is so important. It reminds us of our destinies, the legacies we incarnated here to create. Or to simply go within to find answers, finding solace, peace, and wisdom in an often chaotic and distorted world. *Enlightenment* signifies journeying through the darkness to find wisdom, truth, and light in the shadows. We all have a shadow self, toxic and less desirable traits to transcend. Crystals, chakra healing, and astrology can powerfully assist you in rediscovering your truest nature, while aligning you with hidden pearls and gems of ancient wisdom and self-knowledge. *Do you feel more awakened?* I certainly do! I hope you do too.

Remember to apply meditation coupled with the other tools described in this book to your healing journey with crystals and astrology. Sit down in prayer and meditation, create a sacred space, and activate your Higher Self. Set your intentions for the key takeaways to become your daily mantras; affirm them to the universe, and then watch the magic unfold. We're all interconnected!

Your Crystals and Healing Stones Journey Supports Children in Need

Our Commitment to Giving

This book is more than a literary endeavor; it reflects a heartfelt commitment to helping underprivileged children. **100% of the profits** from Lilli's books are donated directly to charitable efforts dedicated to **helping children in need.**

Lilli Abbott's books are published by Mei Service, a boutique publishing house with a vision to help children to learn, one word and one book at a time.

Join Us

To learn more about our initiatives and how your contribution is lighting up young lives, we welcome you to visit us at:

www.meiservicebooks.com

You have embarked on a journey of reading, knowing that your path through these pages helps pave the way for a brighter tomorrow for the young ones we serve.

Together, let's turn the act of reading into a legacy of hope.

If you have enjoyed this book, please check out other books in the series, *Numerology and Spiritual Healing* and *Astrology and Crystals*. There is much more to explore about gemstones, crystals, and the importance of numbers for each Star Sign!

Mei Service Books

Discover more books written by Lilli Abbott

**Discover a new world, and turn another page!
Start a new journey, and find a favorite read today**

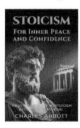 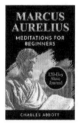

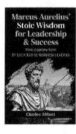 

Get your gift: A Free 90-Day Stoic Journal

About the Author

Lilli Abott is a very passionate explorer of the mystic realms of Astrology and Numerology.

As an author dedicated to the esoteric arts, her writing is a fusion of celestial wisdom and numerical insights. From horoscopes that illuminate the path of your Sun sign to in-depth analyses of the numerical vibrations that influence our existence, Lilli's work is a celestial roadmap guiding you toward self-discovery and personal growth.

Lilli grew up in Los Angeles and studied Psychology at UCLA (University of California-Los Angeles).

Please Leave a 5-star Review

If you enjoyed this book, please leave a positive review to help more readers discover *Crystals and Healing Stones.*

Made in United States
Troutdale, OR
05/17/2024

19948412R00062